After the Goodbye

Holding Love, Releasing Guilt, and Loving Forward After Child Loss

Maureen C. Rubalcaba, PhD

DEDICATION

For my son,

Michael Simon Chavez...the light that forever changed me, the love that time could not silence, and the heartbeat that guides every word I write.

For my children,

Melissa, Alicia, Isabela, Carlos, and Emiliano...each of you carry a piece of Michael's light within you. Your laughter has mended some of what grief once broke. Your love has taught me how to live again, to mother again, and to honor your brother not in sorrow, but in the way we love one another, fully and fiercely.

And for my husband,

Johnny "Juan" Rubalcaba...your steadfast love has been the ground beneath feet, the quiet strength that held me when I could not stand. You have walked beside me through every shadow, reminding me that love is not diminished by grief, but deepened by it.

This book exists because love refused to die. It is a hymn for the child I carry in my soul, and a testament to the community who helped me keep breathing when my world went silent.

Contents

FORWARD

For Michael Simon Chavez, my beloved son, my teacher in love beyond life, and the heartbeat behind every word that follows. When Michael died, the world went silent, not just in sound, but in spirit. That silence changed everything about who I was, how I saw the world, and what I came here to do. Out of that silence and the finality of our goodbye grew this book.

It is not a story about moving on but about living within. It is a letter of love to every parent who wakes up to an empty room, a missed phone call or text, or the aching space where laughter used to be. It is proof that love does not end, it transforms.

Michael's life was short, but his impact is eternal. He remains the center of my purpose and the reason I reach back for others lost in the dark. His love made me who I am; his absence made me listen more deeply to what love can do. In the early days after Michael's death, I could barely breathe. My body remembered him before my mind could catch up. But over time, through tears, reflection, and connection with others who walk this road, I discovered something sacred: grief and love are not opposites. They are two halves of the same heartbeat.

Michael taught me that love does not fade; it evolves. He is still here, in every thought, with every parent I sit beside, every word I write to remind the grieving that they are not broken. This book was born from that truth.

And though my arms could no longer hold him, they have held his siblings; Melissa, Alicia, Isabela, Carlos, and Emiliano with fierceness and tenderness born from that same unending love. Their laughter, their presence, and their faith in me became the bridge between the life I lost and the life I chose to keep living. Through them, I learned that love for Michael could continue to grow, not only in memory, but in motion, in family, and in the everyday moments that tether me to both heaven and earth. Their love is my reminder that Michael's story lives on through all of us

To every parent who finds themselves reading these pages, may you feel less alone in your pain, and more seen in your love. May you come to know that you are still a parent, that your love still matters, and that your child's life, held in love rather than counted in time, continues to shape this world through you.

This book is for him. And it is for them, my children who have walked beside me in love and in light. It is for you, because you, too, are still loving, still breathing, still carrying your child forward. You can navigate your grief without guilt or fear of judgment to release self-blame and love forward with purpose and meaning after child loss.

Dr. Maureen C. Rubalcaba, PhD
Bereaved Parent, Mother to Michael Simon Chavez

AFTER THE GOODBYE: HOLDING LOVE, RELEASING GUILT, AND LOVING FORWARD AFTER CHILD LOSS

February 7, 1995, is the day the world shifted beneath my feet and never returned to the way it was. The night before, I was Michael's mother in the way every mother knows herself to be planning his next feeding, memorizing the sound of his breath, holding his tiny fingers in mine. By the early morning, I was still a mom, but now I carried a weight no parent should ever know: my son was gone. Sudden Infant Death Syndrome (SIDS) had taken him quietly, without warning, leaving a silence so loud it rattled through my bones.

The hours that followed were a blur of disbelief and shattered dreams. My arms ached with an emptiness no one could see, and my heart tried to make sense of something that will never make sense. People told me I was strong. I did not feel strong. I felt broken, stripped bare, left in a world where the sun still rose even though mine had set.

Grief became my shadow. Some days, it pressed down so heavily I wondered how I could keep breathing. Other days, it was a faint whisper in the background, reminding me of love so deep it could not be undone. Surviving grief is not a single act, it is waking up each day and choosing, in some small way, to keep going. It is learning to live in a world that no longer has your child but still carries the imprint of their life in everything you do.

To every parent reading this who has lost their precious child, I need you to know this, you are not alone in this storm. I carry my grief for Michael every day; sometimes as a heavy stone in my pocket, sometimes as a tender memory that catches the light. This chapter is my story of love, loss, and the complicated, messy, sacred work of surviving and navigating grief. It is my way of reaching for your hand to say "I see you. I honor your grief. And even in the darkest nights, you are not walking them alone."

A Companion for the Unthinkable

When a child dies, a parent does not just grieve a life lost, they grieve the version of themselves who existed before the loss. The world becomes unfamiliar, their identity shatters, and even their body remembers the absence. Every breath, every sunrise, every quiet moment becomes a confrontation with the impossible question: How do I keep living when my child does not? This is not emotional pain. This is existential disorientation.

It touches every layer of who you are: your sense of identity, your sense of safety, your sense of belonging, your relationship to time, your relationship to love. Society is deeply uncomfortable with grief, especially the grief of child loss. Friends fall silent. People say the wrong things or disappear entirely. Bereaved parents often feel exiled from the world they once belonged to. Your grief becomes too heavy, too much, too long for others. The result is a loneliness that cuts to the bone, even in rooms full of people.

Cultural narratives about grief are impatient and unrealistic. Parents are told to be grateful for other children, to get back to work, to find closure. But closure does not exist. What these parents need is continuing bonds, a way to stay connected to their child with love, without apology.

The world no longer makes sense. Faith may falter, relationships may strain, and even joy can feel like betrayal. Grieving parents often struggle to rebuild meaning, to find purpose that honors their child's life while accepting their own continued existence.

Perhaps the most haunting fear is that their child will be forgotten by others, by the world, even by themselves. Parents long for acknowledgment that their child was here, mattered, and still does.

At the heart of this problem is a paradox every bereaved parent lives with "I am forever changed by love and loss. I must learn to be a parent in absence, to love in a world that cannot see my child."

If you are holding this, you have taken a courageous step into a landscape that feels isolating and unbearable. This is not a book to get over grief, but a companion for the days when taking another breath feels like a victory. It is an invitation to witness one mother's walk-through loss to learn to live within it. If you feel broken, heart, body, and soul, there is nothing wrong with you; it means you are grieving. This space is for you, to honor your story, your child, and the love that remains.

You are seen and you are not walking these darkest nights alone.

Finding a Language for Loss

Grieving parents are not looking for answers. They are looking for language. For reflection. For belonging. For proof that what they feel is survivable and that love, even after death, still has a place to go.

This book meets bereaved parents exactly where they are, inside the ache, not beyond it. It offers validation, permission to feel everything without judgment or timeline. It offers visibility, to see themselves in my story and realize they are not alone. It offers voice, words for the pain they have struggled to express. It offers vision, glimpses of how love continues to evolve long after loss.

This is a real-time account of the life sentence of grief and how to survive the unthinkable. You will see how grief is not an ending but a change of love. You will find words for feelings that are impossible to speak, like the ache in my arms and the experience of losing her too, the mother I once was. You will discover that your love for your child is not a memory to be preserved, but an active, living force you carry forward into everything you do.

What I came to understand is that love does not end when a child dies. It persists with quiet determination, steady and unyielding. It does not fade with time or distance. Instead, it threads itself into every part of who you are, until loving them feels as instinctive and necessary as breathing.

At first, I thought keeping Michael close meant refusing to move forward. I worried that if I smiled too much or laughed too easily, I would somehow betray him. But slowly, I realized that the love I had for him was not asking me to stop living, it was asking me to carry him with me into everything I did.

I noticed the ways he still showed up. In the winter sun pouring through my window, in the quiet of the early morning, in the random appearance of a butterfly when I needed it most. I did not go looking for these moments, they found me. Each one felt like a reminder that Michael was still part of my story, even if not in the way I had imagined.

I kept pieces of him close. His blanket. The outfit he wore home from the hospital, a photograph that captured the softness in his cheeks. I talked to him when I was alone, telling him about my day, my fears, my love. These rituals are my lifeline. They do not erase the ache, but they give me a way to keep him present in my life.

Over time, I began to see that loving him after death is not a burden, it is a privilege. My grief is proof that he had lived and mattered, that his short life had changed me forever. That love began to guide my choices; from the way I showed up for others to the way I began speaking openly about child loss.

Carrying Michael forward became less about holding on to the pain and more about honoring his life. Every time I share his story, I feel him near. Every time I offer comfort to another grieving parent, I know I am giving from the love he gave me. That love did not die with Michael. It is alive in me still, shaping the person I have become and the work I am here to do.

This is a testament to survival, offering the fragile, necessary hope that it is possible to live after such a loss. The path forward involves learning to carry your child with you, always, and forging a new identity from the wreckage with their love as your guide.

The Path We Will Walk Together

We will begin in the immediate aftermath when the world falls silent and survival is measured breath by breath. We will navigate the shattering of identity, the physical pain of loss, and the challenge of holding beautiful memories alongside traumatic ones. From there, we will see how love continues after death and how grief does not shrink, but rather, you grow a new life around it. You will learn the importance of finding your people, speaking your child's name, and actively carrying them forward.

In the beginning, survival was not measured in days or weeks. It fractured into minutes. Some mornings, the only thing I could manage was opening my eyes and taking a single breath. Then another. And another. Each one felt like an act of defiance against the crushing weight of my grief.

Time lost all meaning. Hours bled into one another, and I often did not know if it was morning or night. The world outside my window kept moving; people went to work, children played in yards, the sun rose and set, but I remained frozen in the moment when Michael's absence first took hold.

There were moments when the ache in my arms became almost unbearable. I would catch myself instinctively reaching for him, my muscles still remembering the shape and weight of his tiny body. It was a cruel trick of the body, to long for something so deeply that even your bones remember it, but to know it will never come.

People said the wrong things without meaning to. They told me Michael was in a better place or that time would heal. But I did not want him to be in a better place. I wanted him here. And I knew instinctively that time was not going to erase this pain, it was only going to change the way I carried it.

Grief did not make me quieter; it made the world louder in ways I did not ask for. Conversations echoed. Silence rang. My body existed somewhere between shutdown and overstimulation, unable to find a safe place to land. There were moments when my small apartment felt too big, and others when it felt like it was closing in on me. The air carried his absence in ways that words never could. Every room felt stretched thin by the space where he should have been. People wanted to give me explanations. Reasons. Comfort. But I was not looking for any of those. I was looking for something steady. Something human. Something that could sit beside me in the middle of the unbearable without trying to clean it up.

That is when she came... In the blur of days and weeks after Michael's death, when I could barely tell day from night, there was one steady presence who kept showing up, Penny, my Public Health Nurse. Penny was not just a nurse. She was a lifeline. She came into my home not with the sterile detachment I expected, but with the quiet, steady compassion of someone who understood that grief lived in the air and on the skin.

She never rushed me. Never asked me to tidy up the mess of my house or my soul. Penny sat in the middle of my shattered life without trying to fix it. She listened when the words poured out fast and raw, and she listened when all I could do was cry. She did not flinch at the weight of my grief. Somehow, her presence made it feel just a little less unbearable.

Through Penny, I learned there were other parents who had walked this same road, parents whose arms ached like mine, whose hearts knew the unnatural rhythm of loving a child who no longer breathed. At first, I could not face them. Meeting them would make it too real, and I was still clinging to the thin hope that reality might somehow undo itself. But Penny kept gently telling me, they will understand in a way no one else can.

It took years, seven long, aching years, before I found the courage to attend my first SIDS conference. By then, I had learned to function in the world again, at least on the outside. But inside, the roller coaster of grief never stopped. It was relentless, the sharp drops into despair, sudden jolts of fear, moments of guilt that slammed into me without warning. The idea of walking into a room full of other bereaved parents terrified me. I was afraid it would pull me back under, afraid the pain would consume me all over again.

But the deep truth was this: I was still living in trauma and fear, and I knew that if I did not step toward my grief, it would keep swallowing me whole. I did not go to that conference because I was ready in any traditional sense. I went because I wanted to honor Michael, because hiding from the grief was different from healing with it.

The first moment I walked through the doors, I felt my chest tighten. But then I saw them; parents with eyes that mirrored my own. Eyes that had seen the unthinkable and were still there. We did not need small talk. We did not need to explain. Our grief was the common language, and in it there was both heaviness and relief.

Those few days something cracked open in me. We shared stories of our babies, not just how they died, but who they were. We cried together, and sometimes we laughed. We remembered birthdays, anniversaries, and all the intricate details that made our children real in a world that had moved on. It was the first time I felt I could speak Michael's name freely without making someone else uncomfortable.

Leaving that conference, my heart was still shattered, and the absence of my son remained as permanent as my breath. Nothing about my grief had magically softened. But something subtle yet profound had shifted. I had witnessed my story reflected in the eyes of others who understood this kind of love and loss without explanation. Michael's name was spoken, remembered, and carried by people who had never met him but honored him, nonetheless. In that shared witnessing, I felt the first quiet movement away from simply enduring my grief toward learning how to live alongside it with intention, with reverence, and always in love for my son.

The central lesson is one of enduring connection. The way forward is not built on the hope that grief will disappear. It is shaped by the truth that love endures, steady and unrelenting, carrying us even when the weight feels impossible.

As you move through these pages, you may begin to notice the quiet rhythm of the title itself. After the Goodbye is not a moment; it is a life. It asks you to keep holding love when there is no body to hold, to begin releasing guilt that was never yours to carry, and, in time, to explore what loving forward might mean in a world your child cannot physically walk through. These are not goals or assignments. They are gentle names for the movements your heart is already making, a language to honor what you are living."

WHEN THE WORLD FELL SILENT

The hours after a child's death are a blur, yet sharp in a way that feels burned into the skin. The world slows to half-speed, sounds are muffled, and reality feels like a nightmare you cannot escape. You may find yourself clinging to hope, willing the clock to turn back, only to face the impossible, your child is gone.

This chapter addresses that surreal, crushing weight of sitting in a hospital, surrounded by first responders, while everything inside you screams for a reality that no longer exists. It validates the initial shock, the numbness, and the logistical nightmare of dealing with the mechanics of death while your own world has stopped turning.

It is a space to acknowledge the trauma of those first moments.

The Immediate Aftermath

The hours after Michael's death passed in a distorted haze. Time slowed and fractured, yet every detail etched itself into my body with a clarity I could not escape. My body still remembers the heavy rain and frigid air that morning, the surreal sight of first responders; firefighters, paramedics, and police moving with quiet urgency. It was as if the world had slowed to half-speed, every sound muffled except for the pounding of my own heart.

I held on to the illusion that time might reverse itself, bargaining silently for a different ending, grasping for anything that might undo what had already happened, a miracle. But there was no miracle. There was only the reality that Michael was gone. The words did not make sense at first. They floated in the air around me, heavy and impossible, like trying to breathe underwater.

The physical pain came instantly. My chest felt as though it had been crushed, my arms ached with a hollowness that could not be soothed. My body moved on instinct, reaching for a presence my mind could not yet accept was gone. My whole body screamed for him. Mentally, the world was shattering. There was a ringing in my ears, a dull hum that drowned out voices. People were speaking, asking questions, offering comfort, but their words slid past me, meaningless against the roar of my grief. I kept waiting to wake up, to hear him cry; to realize this was just a bad dream. But reality settled like lead in my bones.

The hospital was cold, and yet I remember sweating, my palms damp as I sat in an open waiting room. I could feel every second passing, each one carrying me further away from the last time I saw my son alive. The sterile scent of antiseptic burned in my nose. The low voices of nurses and the shuffle of footsteps in the hallway made the space feel both too small and endless at the same time.

When they told me it was final, that he was truly gone, I could not move. I could not even cry at first. My whole body locked up, as if refusing to accept what my heart already knew. In that moment, a part of me died with Michael. The life I had known, the mother and woman I had been just hours earlier, was gone in an instant.

Everything after that was motion without meaning; signing forms I could not read, nodding at words I could not hear, walking through hallways that felt a hundred miles long. The only clear truth was this: my arms were empty, and they would be empty for the rest of my life.

If you are in those first hours, those first days, know this, your body and mind are in shock. There is no right way to feel. The numbness, the disbelief, the physical ache, they are all valid responses to an unthinkable reality. You are surviving something that should never happen.

Do not judge your reactions. Allow yourself to feel numb, confused, or nothing at all. When people ask how you are, you do not owe them an answer that makes them comfortable. Your only task right now is to survive this second. Then the next one.

His First Smile, His Last Day

February 6, 1995, began with a miracle. That morning, Michael gave me his very first real smile, a genuine, heart-deep smile that lit up his whole face and wrapped itself around my soul.

He was stubborn and strong, just as he had been from the start. My pregnancy was hard, his delivery abrupt; weeks early, emergency C-section after a failed aversion procedure because he was breech. Born during the holiday season, he was the greatest Christmas gift I could have ever imagined.

On February 7, 1995, in the early morning hours, my arms were empty. The baby boy who had fought his way into this world, the boy whose spirit filled our home, was gone. SIDS had taken him without warning, leaving a silence so deafening it swallowed the air around me.

I can still see it, Michael's tiny face that morning, his eyes bright and curious, his mouth curling into that first true smile. Not the little reflexive grins babies make in their sleep, but one filled with something deeper, something knowing. His lips stretched just enough to show a glimpse of his gums, his cheeks puffed and warm, and his gaze locked onto mine as if we shared a secret.

My heart swelled so full it almost hurt, and I remember thinking, this is what love looks like. I kissed his forehead and held him close, inhaling the sweet, milky scent of his skin. That moment is etched into me, untouched by time.

Hours later, I was in the hospital, sitting in a waiting room that felt both too small and endlessly vast. My body still remembers the weight of that chair, the sterile smell of the air, the low hum of voices I could not quite understand.

I remember the sea of uniforms; firefighters, paramedics, nurses, each one a silent witness to the unraveling of my world. My arms were empty, my chest hollow. I had entered the evening with a smiling baby in my arms and by the next morning I was staring into a reality where I would never again feel the warmth of his little body against mine.

Life can deliver the cruelest kind of whiplash, giving you a perfect moment only to rip it away without warning. That smile, and the hours that followed, live side by side in my memory. One is my proof of his joy, the other my proof of survival. Joy and sorrow become forever connected in your heart. You cannot have one without the other. They rise and fall like the tide, sometimes bringing warmth, sometimes pulling you under. Acknowledging this duality is not a betrayal of your love; it is the truth of your new reality and a testament to the life that was lived, no matter how short.

When memories surface, both joyous and painful, allow them to coexist without forcing one away. Your child's laughter and their last breath are both part of their story. Both are part of yours. The beautiful moments do not make the loss less real. The traumatic moments do not make the love less true. Hold both. They belong together in the sacred space of your heart.

The Physical Pain of Loss

The pain of child loss comes instantly and is deeply physical. Your chest tightens as if under an invisible weight, and your arms carry a quiet, relentless ache; an emptiness shaped by memory, reaching for a child your body still expects to hold. This is the ache in my arms, a physical truth of grief that society often ignores. Your muscles may twitch with the memory of your child's weight, a cruel trick of the body that longs for something so deeply it remembers in every detail. The way their head fits in the crook of your elbow. The feeling of their breath against your neck. The weight of them sleeping on your chest. Your body does not understand that they are gone. It keeps reaching, keeps expecting, keeps preparing for a presence that will never return.

Grief lives in your bones, a constant reminder of the physical emptiness left behind. Some days, the ache is so sharp it takes your breath away. Other days, it is a dull throb that follows you through every movement. You may catch your body reacting before your mind; arms instinctively folding inward, your breath catching at familiar sensations, or your muscles responding to echoes of a presence that once lived within your daily rhythm.

This is not just an emotional experience; it is a full-body reality.

People will tell you that grief is all in your head, but your body knows better. The exhaustion that makes simple tasks feel impossible. The way your chest tightens when you see other children. The physical need to curl up small, as if you could protect what is left of yourself.

Your body is grieving too, and it deserves the same compassion you would give to any other physical wound. When the physical ache in your arms arises, place a hand over your heart and acknowledge it as a physical manifestation of your love. Your body's memory of holding your child is proof of the bond you shared. The pain is real because the love was real.

Rest when you need to rest. Move when movement feels healing. Listen to what your body is telling you about what it needs to survive this. The physical pain of loss is your love made manifest in your bones, muscles, and heartbeat. It is sacred, even when it hurts.

Surviving the Initial Shock

There is a particular kind of silence that descends when your child dies, not the absence of sound, but the absence of what sound used to mean. The world continues its noise around you, yet nothing penetrates the thick wall that now separates you from everything you once understood as normal. You are caught between two impossibilities; the reality that your child is gone, and the reality that you are somehow still here, still breathing, still expected to exist in a world that makes no sense without them.

What you have walked through in these pages is not simply the story of loss. It is the anatomy of shock, that merciful fog that wraps around you in the beginning, protecting you from absorbing the full weight of the unthinkable all at once. You have seen how grief announces itself not just emotionally but physically, how your arms ache with a hollow emptiness that no position can ease, how your chest tightens as if bearing an invisible weight, how your body continues to reach for a presence it remembers in muscle and bone even when your mind knows they are gone.

You have witnessed the strange distortion of time in those early hours and days, how minutes stretch into eternities while entire days vanish without trace. How you can be surrounded by first responders, medical personnel, well-meaning friends, and still feel utterly, devastatingly alone. How the logistics of death, the paperwork, the phone calls, the arrangements, feel surreal and grotesque when set against the enormity of your loss.

Perhaps most important, you have begun to understand that there is no right way to survive this. Your numbness is not failure. Your disbelief is not denial. Your inability to cry, or your inability to stop crying, your need to talk incessantly about your child or your inability to speak their name without choking, none of these responses are wrong. They are simply your body and mind doing whatever they must to survive what should not be survivable.

The beauty and terror of Michael's first smile on his last day of life, this paradox lives at the heart of every bereaved parent's existence. Joy and devastation are not opposites in grief; they are intimate companions, woven so tightly together that you cannot separate one from the other. Learning to hold both, to honor both, without trying to push either away, is one of the first and hardest lessons of this unwanted education.

Your body is not betraying you when it remembers what your mind wishes it could forget. It is bearing witness to the love that existed, to the bond that was real and profound and worthy of this depth of pain. The ache in your arms is sacred. The tightness in your chest is testimony. The exhaustion that makes breathing feel like climbing mountains is your whole being engaged in the monumental work of grieving.

You are not going crazy, even when the world feels unmoored from reality. You are not broken beyond repair, even when you cannot imagine ever feeling whole again. You are in shock, and shock does its work slowly, releasing its hold in layers rather than all at once. This is protection, not pathology. This is your mind and body conspiring to keep you alive when part of you has died.

In these first impossible days, you are learning the difference between surviving and living, and right now, surviving is enough. More than enough. It is everything.

Here are the actionable steps for moving through your grief and surviving the initial shock:

First, do not judge your initial reactions; allow yourself to feel numb, confused, or nothing at all. Your responses are normal reactions to an abnormal situation. There is no timeline for shock to wear off, no right way to process the impossible.

Second, when the physical ache in your arms arises, place a hand over your heart and acknowledge it as a physical manifestation of your love. Say out loud: This pain is proof of how much I love my child. My body remembers because our bond was real.

Third, when memories surface, both joyous and painful, allow them to coexist without forcing one away. Do not try to push away the happy memories because they hurt. Do not try to forget the traumatic moments because they haunt you. Both are part of your child's story and yours.

Fourth, focus only on the immediate moment. Your only task is to survive this second. Not the day, not the week, not the rest of your life. Just this breath. Then the next one. Build your survival one moment at a time.

Fifth, accept help with the planning. Let others manage phone calls, arrangements, paperwork. Your energy is precious and limited. Use it for breathing, for surviving, for honoring your child in whatever small way feels right.

Sixth, create one small ritual that connects you to your child. Hold their blanket. Look at their photo. Say their name out loud. Light a candle. These tiny acts of love can anchor you when everything else feels like it is spinning out of control.

Finally, remember that shock is your mind's way of protecting you from absorbing all the pain at once. It will wear off gradually, and when it does you will feel the full weight of your loss. That is normal. That is part of the process. You are not getting worse; you are beginning to heal.

In these first days and weeks, "After the Goodbye" is not a concept, it is the air you are trying to breathe. Here, holding love looks like staying with yourself for one more second, one more breath, even when you feel undone. Releasing guilt begins quietly, with the radical truth that nothing about your reactions is wrong or too much. Loving forward is not a task for today; it is simply the fact that you are still here, still loving a child this world can no longer see.

The world fell silent when your child died, but your love for them never will. That love will carry you through these first impossible days, one breath at a time. You are not alone in this.

EARLY SURVIVAL: BREATH-BY-BREATH

By then, I had stopped asking how I was supposed to survive it. The question itself felt too big, too heavy, like trying to lift an entire collapsing building with bare hands. Survival was not a plan. It was not even a goal. It had become instinct, something raw and animal inside me that refused to let me completely disappear.

There were days my body moved without my permission. I would find myself standing somewhere in the house with no memory of how I got there. Moments where time folded in on itself and everything felt unreal, like I was watching someone else live my life from a distance.

People around me continued talking about the future. About healing. About strength. But the future meant nothing to me then. All I could see was the space where my son should have been. All I could feel was the quiet violence of having to live when he could not.

I did not learn how to survive all at once. I learned in fragments. In seconds. In breaths. In the decision to stay instead of disappear. And from those fragments, I began to understand that survival had to become something smaller. Something gentler. Something possible.

The Strategy for Impossible Moments

When the future feels unbearable, when the thought of tomorrow makes your chest tighten and your head spin, survival becomes something much smaller and more manageable. The strategy for impossible moments is to shrink your world down to the size of a single breath, a single heartbeat, a single second of existence.

Your energy is precious now, more precious than it has ever been. Before Michael died, I could run on empty for days, pushing through exhaustion with coffee and determination. After he died, making a cup of coffee required planning. Opening the blinds felt like climbing a mountain. The simple act of answering the phone became so overwhelming that I would stare at it ringing, unable to move my hand to pick it up. This is not weakness. This is the heavy work of grieving.

Your body is processing trauma. Your mind is trying to make sense of something that will never make sense. Your heart is learning to beat in a world where your child no longer breathes. Every cell in your body is working overtime to keep you alive when part of you died with your child. Of course you are exhausted. Of course, the simplest tasks feel impossible.

The strategy begins with permission. Permission to do nothing today except exist. Permission to cancel plans, ignore phone calls, and let the dishes sit in the sink. Permission to curl up in your child's room and breathe in whatever remains of their scent. Permission to cry until you have no tears left, or to sit in complete numbness, feeling nothing at all. There is no right way to survive these moments.

When I felt like I could not take another breath, I would break it down even smaller. I would focus on the air entering my nose, filling my lungs, then slowly leaving my body. Just that. Nothing more. The breath became my anchor, the one thing I could control when everything else spun wildly beyond my reach. Sometimes I would count. One breath. Then the next. The counting gave my mind something to do besides scream. The rhythm gave my body something to follow besides the chaos of grief. When even breathing felt too hard, I would focus on something even smaller. The feeling of my feet on the floor. The texture of the blanket against my skin. The sound of the clock ticking on the wall. I would anchor myself to these tiny, concrete realities when the larger reality of Michael's death threatened to pull me under completely.

The impossible moments come in waves. You might be doing fine, relatively speaking, when suddenly the weight of your loss crashes over you like a tsunami. You might be in the grocery store, a school parking lot, or standing in line somewhere ordinary when a sight, a voice, or a moment mirrors your child's life, and suddenly the air leaves your lungs. You might be driving when a song, a phrase, or a passing milestone pulls you back without warning, forcing you to slow down or pull over as grief floods your body and blurs your vision.

These waves do not follow a schedule. They do not care if you are at work, at a family gathering, or trying to sleep. They come when they come, and the strategy is not to fight them but to survive them.

When a wave hits, find the smallest possible task. If you are standing, sit down. If you are sitting, put your hands on your knees. If you cannot do anything else, close your eyes and feel your heart beating. That heartbeat is proof that you are still here, still fighting, still loving your child with every pulse of blood through your veins.

Remember that your child lives in your breath now. Every time you inhale, you breathe life into their memory. Every time you exhale, you send your love out into the world where they exist now, in the space between heartbeats, in the quiet moments between breaths.

The strategy for impossible moments is radical acceptance of your limitations. You cannot do what you used to do. You cannot be who you used to be. You cannot think, feel, or move through the world the way you did before your child died. And that is okay. That is normal. That is the price of loving someone so completely that losing them rewrites every cell in your body.

Your only job right now is to endure. Not to heal, not to move forward, not to find meaning or purpose or hope. Just to endure. To keep breathing when breathing feels impossible. To keep your heart beating when it feels broken beyond repair. To stay in this world when part of you want to follow your child wherever they have gone.

This endurance is not passive. It is the most active, courageous thing you will ever do. Every breath you take is a choice. Every moment you survive is a victory. Every time you open your eyes to face another day without your child, you are doing something extraordinary.

Navigating a World That Doesn't Understand

In early grief, you learn quickly that people will say the wrong things. They will offer platitudes that feel like salt in an open wound. They will tell you that your child is in a better place, that everything happens for a reason, that God needed another angel. These words, meant to comfort, can feel like a deep betrayal because you do not want your child in a better place. You want them here with you.

You will discover that your grief makes others uncomfortable. They want to fix you, to rush you through your pain, to see you return to the person you were before. They do not understand that the person you were before no longer exists. They died with your child.

People will avoid you at the grocery store, cross the street when they see you coming, stop inviting you to gatherings because your presence reminds them that terrible things can happen to good people. Your grief becomes a mirror they do not want to look into because it shows them their own vulnerability, their own fear of losing what they love most.

This abandonment, when it comes, cuts almost as deeply as the original loss.

You need to understand that their discomfort is not your responsibility to manage. You do not have the energy to make others feel better about your tragedy. You do not need to smile and say you are doing fine when you are barely surviving. You do not need to hide your tears, lower your voice when you speak your child's name, or pretend that time is healing wounds that will never fully close.

Your energy is a precious resource, more valuable now than gold, time, or money. Every ounce of it must be reserved for your survival and your grief. You cannot afford to spend it soothing others who are uncomfortable with your pain.

When someone says your child is in a better place, you have permission to say, "I don't want to talk about that right now." When they tell you that time heals all wounds, you can respond with, "That hasn't been my experience." When they suggest that you should be grateful for your other children or that you should move on, you can simply walk away. You do not owe anyone an explanation for your grief.

Some people will surprise you with their capacity for presence. They will sit with you in silence, bring you food without expecting conversation, or simply text you to say they are thinking of you without requiring a response. These people are gifts. Hold onto them. They understand that love sometimes looks like showing up without trying to fix anything.

Others will disappoint you in ways that feel like additional losses. Friends who were once close will fade away. Family members will say hurtful things. People you thought you could count on will prove that they cannot handle the weight of your grief alongside their own lives.

This is not a reflection of your worth or your child's worth. It reflects their limitations, their fear, their inability to sit with pain that has no solution. I built protective barriers around my heart. I thought of these barriers not as walls that keep love out, but as filters that let in only what serves my healing and keeps out what causes additional harm. You have the right to set boundaries; to screen your phone calls, to avoid certain people, to leave gatherings early when the conversation becomes too much.

You have the right to say no to invitations, obligations, and expectations that feel too heavy to carry right now. Your social calendar, your work schedule, your family commitments, all these things can wait while you do the essential work of surviving.

When someone asks how you are doing, you do not need to give them a real answer if you do not want to. "I'm taking it one day at a time" is perfectly acceptable. "It's been really hard" is honest without being overwhelming. "I don't want to talk about it right now" is a complete sentence that requires no further explanation.

You will also encounter people who have walked this path before you. Other bereaved parents who understand the weight you carry, the ache in your arms, the way your child's absence changes everything about how you move through the world. These people are treasures. When you find them, or when they find you, let them in. They will not try to fix your grief or rush you through it. They will simply witness it, honor it, and remind you that you are not alone.

The world does not understand that grief is not a problem to be solved but a love to be carried. It does not understand that your sadness is not depression but devotion. It does not understand that speaking your child's name is not dwelling on the past but keeping them present in your life.

You do not need the world to understand. You need only a few people who get it, who can sit with you in the darkness without trying to turn on the lights, who can hear your child's name without flinching, who can let you cry without offering tissues or solutions.

Your grief is not too much. Your love is not too big. Your child's life, no matter how short, mattered immensely. Anyone who cannot hold space for these truths is not worthy of your precious energy. Save your strength for the people who show up without conditions, who love you through the mess, who understand that supporting you means supporting your right to grieve fully and completely, for as long as it takes.

Finding Your Smallest Victories

Hope for the future is an impossible concept in the beginning. The idea of tomorrow, let alone next year or the rest of your life, feels overwhelming and pointless. How can there be a future when your child is not in it? How can you plan for days that will never include their laughter, their growth, their presence?

Survival after child loss is rarely dramatic or visible. It is measured in moments so small they might go unnoticed by anyone else. Opening your eyes and choosing to rise is an act of bravery. Letting warm water fall over you while tears come uninvited is not weakness, it is persistence. Stepping outside, even briefly, to feel air on your skin is not insignificant; it is proof that you are still here, still trying, still honoring life in the only ways you can. These quiet acts are not minimal, they are monumental. These small acts become the fragile scaffolding you will one day stand on to start living again.

I remember the first time I made myself a cup of coffee after Michael died. It sounds so simple, so ordinary, but it required a series of decisions and actions that felt enormous. I had to decide I wanted coffee. I had to get out of bed, walk to the kitchen, find the coffee, measure it, add water, wait for it to brew. Each step felt impossibly heavy, as though my body and mind were moving through thick resistance just to complete something so ordinary.

When I finally held that warm cup in my hands, I cried. Not because I was sad, though I was, but because I had done something normal, something that connected me to the person I used to be, something that proved I was still capable of taking care of myself in the smallest way.

That cup of coffee was a victory.

Your victories might look different. Maybe it is brushing your teeth. Maybe it is changing out of the clothes you have been wearing for three days. Maybe it is answering one text message or eating something other than crackers. Maybe it is looking at a photo of your child without completely falling apart.

These victories do not erase your grief. They do not mean you are getting better or moving on. They simply mean you are surviving, and survival is the most important work you can do right now.

Some days, your victory might be as small as opening the curtains. Light coming into your space can feel like too much when you are deep in grief, but it can also remind your body that the world still exists, that there is still beauty and warmth even in your darkest moments.

Other days, your victory might be taking a shower. The warm water can feel healing, washing away some of the heaviness you carry. Or it might make you cry harder as you remember bathing your child, but even crying can be a victory when it helps you release some of the pressure building inside your chest. Sometimes your victory will be eating something nourishing. Grief often steals your appetite, making food taste like cardboard or making your stomach reject everything you try to consume. But your body needs fuel to do the work of grieving, to keep your heart beating, to maintain the strength required for survival.

One of the most important victories is saying your child's name out loud. The world might want you to stop talking about them, to move past their memory, but speaking their name is an act of love and defiance. It declares that they existed, that they mattered, that their life had meaning.

When I said "Michael" out loud for the first time after he died, it felt like I was bringing him back into the room with me. His name on my lips was a bridge between the world where he lived and the world where he exists now, in memory and love.

Another victory is asking for help when you need it. Pride becomes a luxury you cannot afford in early grief. If someone offers to bring you groceries, let them. If they offer to sit with you while you cry, accept their presence. If they offer to manage phone calls or arrangements, give them permission to lighten your load. Accepting help is not weakness. It is wisdom. It is recognizing that you cannot do this alone, that community and support are essential for survival.

Some victories are internal. Maybe you have a moment where you remember your child and smile instead of only feeling pain. Maybe you realize that their love is still with you, still real, still guiding your choices even though they are physically gone. Maybe you have a moment of gratitude for the time you had together. This does not mean you are glad they died or that you have accepted their death. It simply means you can hold both grief and gratitude in the same space, acknowledging that their life, no matter how short, was a gift.

Your victories might include finding one perfect memory to hold onto during the hardest moments. For me, it was Michael's first and only smile, the way his whole face lit up, and his eyes locked onto mine. When the grief threatened to pull me under completely, I would close my eyes and return to that moment, letting it anchor me to love instead of only pain.

Keep a mental list of these small victories. On the days when you feel like you are not making any progress, when the grief feels as fresh and overwhelming as it did in the beginning, remember what you have already survived.

Remember the cup of coffee, the shower, the moment you spoke their name, the day you got out of bed when staying under the covers felt safer. These victories are proof of your strength, evidence of your love, and the foundation upon which you will slowly, carefully, begin to rebuild a life that honors your child while allowing you to continue living.

The goal is never to get over your grief or to return to who you were before. The goal is simply to endure the next moment, to find the next small victory, to keep breathing until breathing becomes a little easier, to keep loving until that love becomes a source of strength instead of only pain.

Every small victory is a step toward a life where you can carry your child with you always, where their memory becomes a source of comfort instead of only sorrow, where their love guides you forward instead of only holding you back.

Enduring the Next Moment

Survival, you are learning, is not what you thought it would be. It does not arrive as courage or determination or strength of will. It comes as something far more humble and far more profound as breath. As heartbeat. As the simple, animal instinct to remain when every part of you longs to follow your child wherever they have gone.

What you have moved through in this chapter is the terrain between shock and awareness, that terrible season when the protective fog begins to lift and the full weight of loss starts to settle onto your shoulders. You have learned that survival must be measured in increments almost too small to name, not days or even hours, but moments. Seconds. The space between one breath and the next.

You have discovered that the future is not something you can think about right now. The word "tomorrow" feels like a concept from another language, one you no longer speak. Planning ahead, looking forward, imagining a life that extends beyond this present moment of pain, these are luxuries you cannot yet afford. Your only task, your only purpose, is to endure this second. And then the next. And then the one after that.

You have felt how your energy, once abundant, has become the most precious resource you possess. Tasks that were once automatic now require planning, preparation, and decision-making that exhausts you before you even begin. Making coffee. Opening curtains. Answering the phone. Each ordinary action has become extraordinary in its difficulty, not because you are weak but because you are doing the invisible work of keeping yourself alive when part of you has died.

The world's discomfort with your grief has begun to show itself. You have encountered the people who say the wrong things, who offer platitudes that sting rather than comfort, who want to fix your pain or rush you through it or pretend it is smaller than it is. You have felt the peculiar isolation of being surrounded by people who cannot hold space for the depth of your loss, who need you to be better, lighter, more hopeful than you are capable of being right now.

But you have also begun to identify your smallest victories. Those moments of endurance that no one else may notice but that cost you everything. Getting out of bed when staying under the covers felt safer. Eating something, anything, when food tasted like cardboard. Speaking your child's name out loud when silence felt like erasure. Taking a shower. Opening a window. Accepting help. These are not small things. These are the fragile building blocks of survival.

You have learned that your grief makes others uncomfortable not because you are too much, but because they are afraid. Your loss forces them to confront their own vulnerability, to acknowledge that terrible things happen to good people for no reason at all. Their discomfort is not yours to manage. Their inability to witness your pain without flinching is not your responsibility to fix. You do not owe the world a grief that is small enough to be comfortable.

The breath-by-breath survival strategy you are learning now is not just about getting through these early days. It is teaching you a fundamental truth that will serve you for the rest of this journey: when the whole of grief feels impossible to bear, you can bear this moment. This breath. This heartbeat. And from these tiny victories, slowly, so slowly, you will build a life that can hold your loss without being destroyed by it.

You are also learning the crucial skill of protecting your energy, of building boundaries around your wounded heart. You are learning that you have the right to say no, to walk away, to refuse conversations and relationships that drain you rather than sustain you. You are learning to distinguish between people who show up to support you and people who show up to feel better about themselves, between those who can sit with your pain and those who need to fix it.

In this season of breath-by-breath survival, loving forward means nothing more and nothing less than staying. Staying alive. Staying present to your grief. Staying connected to the child you can no longer hold. It is not about healing or moving on or finding silver linings. It is simply about enduring with as much gentleness toward yourself as you can manage.

Here are the specific actionable steps for enduring the next moment:

When you feel overwhelmed, consciously focus on taking one single breath in and out. Make that your only goal. Count if it helps: breathe in for four counts, hold for four counts, breathe out for four counts. Repeat until the wave passes. This breath is your anchor when everything else feels chaotic.

Identify one smallest victory for each day, such as drinking a glass of water, opening the curtains, or stepping outside for thirty seconds. Acknowledge this as proof of your strength. Write it down if you can, creating a record of your courage for the days when you feel like you are not making progress.

Prepare a simple phrase to use when people offer painful platitudes or try to rush your grief. Practice saying: "Thank you, but I'm not ready to talk about that," or "That hasn't been my experience," or simply "I need to go now." You do not owe anyone explanations for your grief or comfort for their discomfort.

Keep one sensory memory of your child close at all times. A scent, a photo, a piece of clothing, a sound recording. When the grief threatens to overwhelm you completely, return to this memory as your anchor. Let it remind you that your love is real, permanent, and stronger than death.

Create a mental or physical list of people who can truly support you without trying to fix your grief. These are the ones who can sit with you in silence, who do not flinch when you say your child's name, who understand that your tears are not a problem to be solved but love that needs expression. Reach out to these people when you need witnessing.

Set boundaries around your energy by giving yourself permission to cancel plans, avoid certain people, and say no to obligations that feel too heavy right now. Your social calendar and commitments can wait while you do the essential work of surviving. This is not selfishness; this is wisdom.

When memories of your child surface, both joyful and traumatic, allow them to coexist without forcing one away. Your child's laughter and their last breath are both part of their story and yours. Hold both with equal tenderness, understanding that the beautiful moments do not make the loss less real, and the painful moments do not make the love less true.

Finally, remember that every moment you survive is an act of love for your child. Your continued presence in this world bears witness to the truth that their life mattered and that your bond as parent and child remains intact. You are still loving them through breath, through memory, through the quiet persistence of staying.

The world may have fallen silent when your child died, but your love for them never will. That love will carry you through these impossible moments. Survival is not measured in days or weeks, but in breaths.

Survival at this stage is not about healing or moving forward. It is about enduring with love as your guide, letting that love be both your anchor in the storm and your compass toward whatever comes next. You are not alone in this.

THE UNRAVELING OF SELF

Child loss does not just break your heart; it fractures your sense of self in ways that are impossible to understand until you live through them. The woman who woke up on February 6, 1995, believing in a safe, predictable world where parents keep their babies and love protects what matters most, vanished the moment Michael took his last breath. She became a ghost I could never become again, a memory of innocence I could observe but never reclaim.

This unraveling happens instantly and completely. One moment you know exactly who you are: a parent, a protector, someone who can kiss away pain and make everything better with your presence. The next moment, you are living in someone else's body, moving through a world that feels alien and unsafe, where the simplest tasks like buying groceries become unbearable reminders of everything you have lost.

The shattering goes deeper than grief for your child, though that grief is the earthquake that splits everything else apart. You find yourself mourning not just the child who died, but the parent you were before, the future you had planned, the person who believed certain tragedies happened to other people. This is the grief that has no name, the loss that society does not acknowledge: the death of the person you used to be.

Every corner of your home feels haunted by the life you were supposed to have. The bedroom that should be filled with toys and laughter sits empty and silent. The routines that once defined your days, feeding schedules and naptime rituals and bedtime stories, are ripped away without warning, leaving gaping holes where purpose used to live. You wake up each morning and for a split second forget, reaching for the monitor or listening for crying before reality crashes down again like a wave you cannot escape.

This unraveling is not a sign of weakness or mental illness, though it may feel like both. It is the natural response of a heart and mind trying to process something that should never happen. Your world is no longer safe, and you cannot trust yourself within it. Every belief you held about fairness, about how life works, about what parents are supposed to protect their children from, lies in pieces around your feet.

Grieving the Person You Were Before Loss

In the days and weeks after Michael's death, I began to realize I was not only grieving my son. I was grieving myself, the woman I had been before the day Michael died, who vanished the moment he took his last breath. She did not walk out slowly or fade away over time; she was gone in an instant, leaving behind a stranger I did not recognize in the mirror.

I could still see her in my memory, the young mother with a heart full of plans and a life full of color. She believed in happy endings and safe spaces and the power of love to protect what mattered most. She thought she understood what loss meant because she had experienced disappointments and setbacks and the normal sorrows that come with being human. She had no idea that real loss could reach inside you and rearrange every atom of your being, leaving you fundamentally changed at the cellular level.

That woman was unreachable now, separated from me by an experience so profound it created an unbridgeable canyon between who I was before and who I would have to become. I felt like I was living in someone else's body. My hands moved and my mouth spoke, but nothing felt real or familiar. The voice that came out when I tried to talk sounded hollow and foreign. The face looking back at me from the bathroom mirror belonged to someone I had never met, someone whose eyes held knowledge I never wanted to possess.

The routines that had once defined me were suddenly absent, creating a disorienting emptiness where structure used to exist. I would wake up at three in the morning, my body still programmed for feeding time, my breasts heavy with milk for a baby who would never drink it again. I would find myself standing in the doorway of his room, listening for sounds that would never come, reaching for tasks that no longer existed.

Grief reshaped my relationship with even the smallest tasks, turning everyday actions into moments that demanded far more energy and intention than I recognized myself having. Grocery stores felt unbearable because passing the baby aisle was like being stabbed in the chest with every step. I would stand frozen in front of the formula and diapers, watching other parents make their selections with casual ease, and wonder how they could move through the world without understanding how fragile it all was, how quickly everything could be taken away.

Holidays became landmines scattered throughout the calendar. Christmas, which had been magical when Michael was born during the holiday season, now felt like a cruel joke. Mother's Day arrived like a slap across the face, a reminder that I was still a mother but could no longer mother to one of my children I loved so much. Even ordinary days could become unbearable when a memory would surface without warning, showing me glimpses of the life I was supposed to be living.

Laughter felt like a betrayal, as if joy meant I was leaving Michael behind or forgetting the weight of what had happened. When something funny occurred and I caught myself almost smiling, guilt would crash down immediately, whispering that good mothers do not find anything amusing when their babies are dead. The woman I had been before would have laughed easily and often; this new version of myself felt like she had forgotten how.

I began to understand that child loss does not just break your heart; it fractures your sense of self so completely that you must learn how to exist all over again. Every belief I had about safety and fairness and the way life works was shattered. My world was no longer predictable or safe. I could not trust it, and I could not trust myself within it, because if something this unthinkable could happen, then anything could happen at any time.

Before loss, the woman I was moved through the world with an unexamined faith that love was a kind of shield, that devotion could outrun disaster, and that motherhood came with an unspoken promise of protection no one ever told me could be broken. She had faith in the natural order of things, in the idea that children outlive their parents and that some tragedies only happen in movies or to people she would never meet. That woman was gone now, and in her place stood someone who knew too much about how suddenly everything can change, how powerless we really are, how little control we have over the things we love most.

Looking back now, I can see that this unraveling was part of the survival process, though at the time it felt like I was losing my mind along with everything else. In losing Michael, I was stripped down to the rawest version of myself, forced to question everything I thought I knew about who I was and what I believed. I had no choice but to slowly rebuild, piece by jagged piece, from whatever remained after the earthquake of his death.

But in those early months, all I knew was that I did not yet know if the one left behind could survive. I was caught between two worlds, the one where Michael had lived and I had been his mother in all the ways that mattered, and this new one where I had to learn how to be his mother in ways I never wanted to know. The bridge between those worlds was made of grief and love and the slow, painful work of accepting that I would never be the same person again.

This grief for the woman I used to be was different from my grief for Michael, but it was connected in ways I could not untangle. I mourned her innocence, her certainty, her ability to move through the world without carrying the weight of knowing that the worst thing imaginable could happen. I missed her laughter, her plans for the future, her belief that love was enough to keep the people she cared about safe.

She had been a good mother, that woman I used to be. She had loved Michael with everything she had, had tried to protect him in all the ways she knew how. But she had not known about SIDS, had not understood that sometimes babies die for no reason that makes sense, had not realized that all the love in the world cannot always prevent the unthinkable from happening.

Grieving her felt necessary but also selfish, like I was taking time and energy away from grieving Michael to mourn someone who seemed less important by comparison. But I came to understand that survival would require becoming someone new.

Losing Yourself Too: A Separate, Connected Loss

The specific grief for the parent you once were and the future you planned must be named and honored as its own distinct loss. This is the grief of losing them too, the person who existed before your child died, and it deserves recognition as a separate but deeply connected tragedy that happened alongside the death of your child.

Your parenthood did not end when your child died. It changed form, not meaning. It transformed into something you never asked for and never wanted to become. You are now a parent who must love their child without the gift of holding them, who must parent through memory instead of presence, who must carry your child forward in ways that feel impossible and inadequate compared to the life you were supposed to share together.

Loss dismantles the architecture of your days without warning. The habits that once anchored you; feeding, soothing, watching, waiting disappear overnight, leaving time unmoored and purpose fractured. You wake to a silence your body does not recognize. Your arms still rise out of instinct. Your body continues to respond as a parent, holding memory in muscle and reflex even as the daily acts of parenting have been taken from you. This dissonance between what your body remembers and what your life now reflects creates a grief that lives everywhere at once: in the heart, the breath, the nervous system. And slowly, painfully, another truth begins to surface beneath the ache of your child's absence. Not only have you lost your child, but you have lost the version of yourself who existed before the world broke. This, too, is a death, one that often goes unnamed.

Every corner of your home can feel haunted by the life you were supposed to have. The rooms that should be filled with toys and milestones sit frozen in time, a museum to dreams that will never unfold. The empty chair at the table. Their clothes hang in the closet, their shoes never to be worn again. You could once move through ordinary places without your body collapsing into memory, without a sound, a face, or a moment pulling you back into the life you were supposed to keep living with your child.

You find yourself avoiding places that remind you of the parent you used to be or the parent you were becoming. Playgroups may feel impossible. The pediatrician's office becomes a place of torture. Driving passed a school as the students leave for the day or a friend's son or daughter graduates from college ignites a flood of emotions. Even the grocery store can trigger overwhelming waves of grief when you see other parents shopping with their children, moving through their lives with the casual confidence you once possessed but will never feel again.

This is a separate but connected loss because the person you were before and the child you lost are forever intertwined in your heart and memory. They were the ones who heard your baby's heartbeat for the first time, counted contractions, and breathed through labor, held your child for those precious hours or days or months when everything felt possible and safe. They were the ones who made plans and bought clothes. They imagined a lifetime of birthdays, graduations, and a wedding day that will never come.

Grieving for them, the person who believed certain losses were unimaginable because they had never lived through them, is not selfish or self-indulgent. It is a vital part of understanding the full scope of what was taken from you on the day your child died. That rupture did not only take your child, but it also altered your internal landscape, dismantling the assumptions you once held about safety, fairness, and how the world was supposed to work, leaving you to navigate life with an awareness that innocence does not survive this kind of loss.

You were the one who could laugh without guilt, who could make plans for next week and next year without the constant awareness that everything could change in an instant. They could watch other people's children without feeling like they were being stabbed in the heart. They could move through ordinary places like grocery stores, schools, parking lots without their body collapsing into memory at the sound of a child's voice, a familiar laugh, a milestone moment, or a glimpse of someone who looked like the child they lost, reminders that now send them spiraling back into absence all over again. Those parents had hopes and dreams that extended beyond survival. They thought about career goals and vacation plans and what kind of parents they wanted to be as their

child grew up. They imagined bedtime stories, milestone celebrations, teaching their child how to ride a bike, or helping their child choose a college. They planned for a future that included watching their child become an adult, maybe even becoming a grandmother someday.
All those dreams died with your child, and the parent who dreamed them died too. In their place stands someone who has been fundamentally altered by loss, someone who knows things they never wanted to know, someone who must learn how to live in a world that no longer makes sense according to the rules they used to believe in.

This new person, the one you are becoming in the aftermath of loss, is not better or worse than the one who came before. They are simply different, forged in the fire of unimaginable grief, shaped by love that has nowhere to go except into memory and ritual and the slow work of carrying your child forward in ways you never planned to learn.

They are stronger in some ways, more aware of what really matters, less likely to take the ordinary miracles of daily life for granted. But they are also more fragile, more easily triggered by reminders of loss, more conscious of how quickly everything can be taken away. They move through the world differently, with a heightened awareness of suffering and a deeper capacity for compassion, but also with a wariness that will never fully disappear.

Learning to honor both of them, the one who came before and the one who remains, is part of the complex work of grieving. You can miss who you used to be while also acknowledging the strength and wisdom that have emerged from your loss. You can grieve for the innocence that died with your child while also recognizing the depth of love and resilience that survival has revealed.

The future you planned with your child is gone, and that deserves its own mourning. The first days of school, holidays, or wedding dances that will never happen represent a lifetime of losses that extend far beyond the initial death. These dreams did not just disappear; they were actively destroyed, leaving you to rebuild not just your daily life but your entire sense of what the future might hold.

Losing them too means acknowledging that you will never be the same person you were before your child died, and that this transformation, while it may eventually bring gifts of wisdom and compassion, was not chosen and is not welcome. It means recognizing that survival requires becoming someone new, someone who can carry impossible grief while still finding ways to live, someone who can love a child who is no longer physically present while also remaining open to whatever form of life becomes possible in the aftermath of loss.

Rebuilding From the Jagged Pieces

The unraveling of your identity strips you down to the rawest version of yourself, leaving you standing in the wreckage of everything you thought you knew about who you were and how the world works. From this place of complete devastation, you have no choice but to slowly rebuild, piece by jagged piece, understanding that the process will be nothing like putting together a puzzle where all the pieces fit neatly and the picture on the box shows you what the finished product should look like.

At first, all you know is that the person you were is gone, and you do not know if the one left behind can survive. You are caught between two impossible realities; the life you lived before, which now feels like it belonged to someone else entirely, and this new existence where your child is dead and you must somehow continue breathing, continue moving, continue finding reasons to open your eyes each morning and face another day in a world that no longer includes their physical presence.

The process is not about finding your old self, because that person no longer exists and cannot be resurrected. They died with your child, and trying to bring them back is like trying to rebuild a house that has been completely destroyed by using only the foundation. The structure that remains cannot support the same building; it must become something entirely different, something that can bear the weight of loss while still providing shelter for the life you must somehow continue living.

This rebuilding involves questioning every belief you had about fairness, safety, and how life works. The assumptions that once formed the bedrock of your existence have been shattered, leaving you to examine each piece and decide what still holds truth and what must be discarded as the naive hopes of someone who had never experienced real loss. You must learn to live with uncertainty as a constant companion, accepting that safety is an illusion and that the people you love can be taken from you without warning or reason.

The work is slow and painful, requiring you to sit with discomfort that feels unbearable while gradually building tolerance for a reality that contradicts everything you once believed about how the world should work. Some days you will feel like you are making progress, finding small pieces of meaning or moments of peace that suggest healing might be possible. Other days you will feel like you are back at the beginning, overwhelmed by grief so fresh it takes your breath away and makes you wonder if you have learned nothing at all about how to survive this.

You must accept that you are permanently changed, that the new person you become will be forged in the fire of this loss and shaped forever by a love that endures beyond death. This is not a temporary transformation that will fade with time; it is a fundamental alteration of who you are at the cellular level. Your DNA has been rewritten by grief,

your nervous system rewired by trauma, your heart expanded by a love so deep it cannot be contained by the boundaries of life and death.
The rebuilding happens in layers, like sediment depositing over time to create new land. Some days you add tiny fragments: the ability to drink coffee without crying, the strength to answer the phone when a friend calls, the courage to say your child's name out loud without your voice breaking. Other days the work is internal and invisible: accepting that joy and sorrow can coexist, understanding that loving your dead child does not require you to stop living, recognizing that survival itself is an act of honor for the life that was lost.

You will discover strengths you never knew you possessed alongside vulnerabilities that surprise you with their depth. You may find that you can sit with other grieving parents and offer comfort with a presence that comes from having walked through the fire yourself, while simultaneously being reduced to tears by a commercial on television or a song on the radio that catches you off guard. This is not inconsistency; it is the complex reality of being human in the aftermath of profound loss.

The new identity you are building will include your child in ways you never planned but that feels essential for your survival. They become woven into your daily life through rituals and memories and the conscious choice to carry them forward in everything you do. You learn to parent in absence, to love without touch, to find ways to honor their life while accepting your own continued existence in a world they no longer physically inhabit. You will realize you are not returning to who you had been, you are learning how to live as who you are becoming.

This rebuilding requires tremendous courage because it means accepting that you will never return to the innocence and certainty you once possessed. You must learn to live with questions that have no answers, to find meaning in experiences that feel meaningless, to create purpose from pain in ways that honor both your grief and your love. You must become someone who can hold space for the darkest realities of human experience while still believing that life has value and beauty worth preserving.

The person you become through this process may be unrecognizable to those who knew you before, and even to yourself at times. You may find that relationships change or end because you can no longer pretend that surface conversations and trivial concerns matter in the same way they once did. You may discover that your priorities have shifted so completely that the life you were building before feels like it belonged to a stranger.

But you may also find that this rebuilding brings gifts you never expected: a deeper capacity for compassion, a clearer understanding of what truly matters, an ability to be present with others in their darkest moments because you have learned to navigate your own. You may discover that your love for your child becomes a source of strength rather than only pain, guiding your choices and giving meaning to your continued existence in ways that surprise you with their power and clarity.

The jagged pieces you are working with will never fit together smoothly. There will always be rough edges and spaces where nothing seems to belong, gaps that cannot be filled and scars that mark where the breaking happened. But from these imperfect materials, you can build something that serves your new reality: a life that honors your child while allowing you to continue living, an identity that includes your role as their parent while also encompassing whatever else you choose to become in the aftermath of loss.

This rebuilding is not a project with a completion date or a goal that can be achieved and then maintained. It is an ongoing process that will continue for the rest of your life, adapting and evolving as you learn new ways to carry your love and your grief, as you discover what it means to live fully while honoring someone who cannot live alongside you in the traditional sense.

This work of becoming someone new is part of what it means to live *After the Goodbye*. You are learning how to hold love for the parent you were, for the child you lost, and for the self who is emerging from the wreckage. Releasing guilt here means loosening the belief that you should somehow be who you were before, or that needing to change is a betrayal. Loving forward, in this season, is as simple and as hard as allowing your transformed self to exist, even when you do not yet recognize them.

Forging a New Identity

You have journeyed through one of grief's most disorienting territories, the loss of not only your child but of the person you were before they died. This is the dimension of loss that often goes unacknowledged by others: the death of your former self, the shattering of the identity you once inhabited with such certainty.

They existed, the parent who moved through the world without carrying this knowledge. They believed in safety, in fairness, in the basic order of things. They made plans for the future with the confidence that tomorrow would arrive as expected. They loved their child with the innocent assumption that love could protect them, that being a good parent was enough to keep them safe. When your child died, they died too. And part of what you are grieving is their loss, their innocence, their certainty, their ability to exist in a world that made sense.

You have come to understand that this unraveling is not weakness or breakdown, but the necessary collapse of a structure that cannot hold the weight of what you now know. Every belief you held about how life works, every assumption about what was possible and impossible, every dream you built for your child's future, all of it has shattered. You are left standing in the wreckage, trying to figure out who you are now, in this reality you never wanted and never imagined.

The future you had planned with your child has vanished. Not just the big milestones, birthdays and graduations and weddings, but the small, ordinary moments you never thought to treasure until they were lost. Morning routines. Bedtime stories. The sound of their laughter. The weight of them in your arms. Your identity was woven through with these plans, these roles, these daily rituals. Without them, you must confront the question: who am I now?

You have learned that you cannot simply return to who you were before. That person no longer exists, and the world where they lived is gone. Forward is not about recovery in any traditional sense. You cannot recover what has been irretrievably lost. Instead, you must forge something new from the jagged pieces of who you were, a self that can hold both grief and love, both brokenness and resilience, both the life that was lost and the life you must somehow continue living.

This rebuilding is not a project with a clear endpoint. It is an ongoing process of discovery that will continue for years, perhaps for the rest of your life. You are not becoming who you were before your loss; you are becoming someone entirely new, someone shaped by love that transcends death, by knowledge gained through surviving the unsurvivable, by a depth of compassion that can only come from walking through your own darkness.

The transformation brings unexpected gifts alongside its losses. You are developing a capacity for empathy that reaches into the deepest places of human pain. You are learning what truly matters and what does not. You are discovering reserves of strength you never knew you possessed. You are finding that you can hold space for others in their suffering because you have learned to hold space for your own.

But these gifts do not erase the cost. The person you are becoming is not better than who you were before, just different, changed in ways you never would have chosen. And grieving for your former self, for the innocence and certainty and dreams she carried, is not betrayal. It is necessary. It is real. It is part of the full accounting of what your child's death has taken from you.

You are learning to forge a new identity that makes space for your role as parent to a child who has died, not was but is. You remain their mother, their father, even though you can no longer parent them in physical ways. This role must be reinvented, expressed through memory and ritual, through speaking their name, through carrying them forward in every choice you make. You are realizing what it means to love someone you cannot see, touch, or hold and finding that this love is no less real for being invisible.

Here are the specific actionable steps for forging your new identity:

Write a letter to the person you were before your loss, acknowledging their life, their dreams, their innocence, and their love for your child. Thank them for the time you shared together and gently say goodbye, recognizing that they cannot return but that their love for your child lives on in who you are becoming. Keep this letter as a bridge between who you were and who you are becoming, returning to it when you need to remember that transformation is not betrayal.

Identify one small routine that was part of your old life and make a conscious decision about whether you want to reclaim it, modify it, or let it go completely. This might be a morning coffee ritual, an evening walk, or a weekly phone call with a friend. Whatever you choose, make it intentional rather than automatic, recognizing that you have the power to decide what parts of your former life still serve who you are now.

When you feel lost or confused about who you are becoming, remind yourself with these exact words: I am discovering who I am now. This reframes the disorientation and uncertainty as an active process of growth rather than a permanent state of being broken. Repeat this phrase whenever you feel overwhelmed by the changes happening within you, understanding that confusion is part of the journey rather than evidence that something is wrong.

Name the specific future plans you lost when your child died and allow yourself to grieve for them explicitly. Write down the Christmas mornings that will never happen, the first days of school you will never witness, the graduation ceremonies and wedding dances that exist now only in your imagination. Give these lost dreams their own space for mourning, understanding that grieving for the future you planned is just as important as grieving for the time you had together.

Create a daily practice of consciously carrying your child forward in some small way, whether through speaking their name, looking at their photo, wearing something that reminds you of them, or making a choice you believe would honor their memory. This transforms your role from the parent you were to the parent you are becoming, someone who parents through memory and love rather than through physical presence.

Identify one belief about yourself or the world that has been shattered by your loss and consciously work to rebuild it in a form that can coexist with your new reality. This might be your understanding of safety, fairness, or the meaning of love. Allow this belief to evolve rather than trying to restore it to its original form, recognizing that wisdom often comes through breaking and rebuilding rather than through protection from harm.

Finally, give yourself permission to become someone you do not yet recognize, understanding that this transformation is not a betrayal of who you were before, but an evolution guided by the deepest love you have ever known. Your child's life and death have changed you in ways that will continue to unfold for years to come, and this ongoing transformation is part of how their love continues to shape the world through your continued existence.

The unraveling of self is painful but necessary, stripping away everything that cannot survive the weight of your loss while revealing the unbreakable core of love that will guide your rebuilding. From this foundation, you can forge a new identity that honors both your grief and your resilience, both your brokenness and your strength, both the life that was lost and the life you choose to continue living in their memory. You are not alone in this.

LOVE THAT DOESN'T DIE

Death can take your child's body, but it can never take your love. It took me months to understand this, tangled as it was in guilt and the quiet terror that healing might mean abandonment. In the beginning, after Michael died, I believed love required me to remain anchored in grief, as if moving forward would loosen our bond. I watched myself carefully, afraid that a smile or a moment of laughter might betray the depth of my devotion to him. But love is not pain, even though pain can be evidence of love.

Slowly, through the fog of early grief, I began to realize that the love I had for Michael was not asking me to stop living. It was asking me to carry him with me into everything I did. This love was stubborn and refused to fade. It wove itself into every part of me until it became as natural as breathing, guiding my choices and shaping the person I was becoming.

The core realization of love that does not die is that this love is not a memory to be preserved like a photograph in a drawer, but an active, living force you carry forward into everything you do. It shows up in the way you treat other people, in the causes you choose to support, in the moments when you speak your child's name without apology. It lives in your breath, in your heartbeat, in the conscious choice to honor their life by continuing to live yours.

An Active, Living Force to Carry Forward

In the months after Michael's death, love stopped feeling like something I had to hold onto and began to feel like something that was holding me. It moved quietly, steadily through my days, no longer something I questioned, but something I lived with. His love, and mine for him, became part of my internal rhythm, shaping how I showed up in the world without asking anything of me except honesty.

I began to understand that carrying Michael forward did not require effort or vigilance. It did not demand that I stay frozen in sorrow or measure my moments of lightness. Love was not keeping score. It was simply present allowing me to live, to breathe, to remain connected without having to justify joy or explain grief.

And then there were the moments when he made himself known. In the warmth of winter sunlight across my face. In the stillness of early mornings when the world felt gentle again. In the unexpected arrival of a butterfly at exactly the moment my heart felt heavy. I did not search for these signs; they arrived on their own. Each one reminded me that Michael was not behind me, he was with me, woven into the life I was still learning how to live.

Your love for your child is not something that happened in the past. It is not a feeling you used to have that died with them. It is a living, breathing force that exists in the present moment and will continue to exist for as long as you draw breath. This love is not diminished by death; it is transformed by it, becoming something more concentrated, more intentional, more powerful than it was when it could be expressed through the simple acts of daily care.

When your child was alive, your love showed up in the thousand small acts of protection and nurture that fill a parent's day. Now that love must find new channels, new ways to flow into the world and make a difference. It becomes the force that helps you comfort another grieving parent, the strength that allows you to speak about child loss when others would rather remain silent, the wisdom that guides you toward what really matters when the world tries to distract you with things that do not.

This active love is different from the desperate clinging that can happen in early grief, when you hold onto pain because releasing it feels like abandoning your child. Active love is conscious and intentional. It makes choices based on what would honor your child's memory rather than what would keep you stuck in the darkest corners of your grief.

Active love asks questions like: How can I carry my child's spirit into this conversation? What would they want me to do in this situation? How can I use this opportunity to make their life matter in ways that extend beyond their death? It is love that looks forward while honoring the past, love that creates meaning from loss while never pretending the loss was acceptable or necessary.

Sometimes this love shows up in big ways, like starting a foundation or changing careers to work with bereaved families or becoming an advocate for research or policy changes. But more often, it shows up in small, daily choices: the decision to be kind to a stranger who seems to be struggling, the choice to listen deeply when someone shares their pain, the commitment to speak your child's name in conversations where their memory brings comfort or connection.

This love is also practical. It might guide you to take better care of your health because your body is the vessel that carries your child's memory forward. It might inspire you to nurture relationships that support your healing because isolation serves no one, especially not the child whose love you are trying to honor. It might encourage you to seek professional help when grief becomes too heavy to carry alone, understanding that getting support is not weakness but wisdom.

The shift from passive grief to active love does not happen overnight, and it does not happen in a straight line. There will be days when the love feels buried under layers of pain, anger, and exhaustion. There will be times when you cannot access the energy required to carry anyone forward, when survival itself takes everything, you have. This is normal and expected. Active love does not demand perfection or constant availability. It simply asks that you remain open to the possibility that your child's death can become a source of life and meaning, not just loss.

One of the most powerful ways to activate this love is through storytelling. Every time you share a memory of your child, every time you talk about who they were and what they meant to you, you are bringing them into the present moment. You are making their life real for people who never got to meet them. You are ensuring that their existence continues to have impact on the world, even though their physical presence has ended.

When you tell someone about your child's first smile, their favorite song, the way they felt in your arms, you are not dwelling on the past. You are making the past present, allowing love to flow across the boundary between life and death in ways that honor both your child's memory and your own continued existence. These stories become gifts you can offer to others, proof that love is stronger than death and that lives matter regardless of how long they last.

Active love also means protecting your child's memory from those who would minimize or dismiss it. When someone tells you to move on or suggests that you should stop talking about your child because it makes them uncomfortable, active love gives you the strength to set boundaries. It reminds you that your child's life was real and significant, that your love for them is permanent and valid, and that anyone who cannot honor these truths does not deserve access to your precious energy.

This love becomes a filter through which you make decisions about how to spend your time, who to spend it with, and what causes deserve your attention and support. It helps you distinguish between activities that drain your spirit and those that nourish it, between relationships that honor your whole story and those that only want the parts that make them comfortable.

The beautiful truth about love that does not die is that it grows stronger with practice. The more you consciously choose to carry your child forward, the more natural it becomes. The more you speak their name, share their story, and make choices that honor their memory, the more you discover that this love is not a burden you must bear but a gift you get to give, both to your child and to the world that was blessed by their existence.

Parenting in Absence

The active practice of parenting in absence is a concept the outside world does not understand but is central to a bereaved parent's life. It is how you continue your bond and honor your child's memory. This involves creating rituals that keep them present, like talking to them when you are alone, telling them about your day, your fears, and your love.

It means keeping pieces of them close. A special blanket, a photograph, a favorite shirt, or special outfit. These actions are not about refusing to move on; they are your lifeline, a tangible way to continue your role as their parent. They did not cease to be your child, and you have not ceased to be their parent.

Parenting in absence is the art of loving someone you cannot touch, protecting someone you cannot hold, and guiding someone who exists now only in your heart and memory. It requires learning an entirely new language of love, one that speaks through ritual and remembrance rather than through the daily acts of physical care that once defined your relationship with your child.

This form of parenting begins with the recognition that your role as your child's mother or father did not end when their life did. The love that made you a parent is permanent and unbreakable. What has changed is not the depth of your connection but the methods through which that connection is expressed and maintained. You must learn to parent through presence of a different kind, through intention and memory and the conscious choice to keep your child's spirit alive in your daily life.

The rituals you create become the new routines of your parenting. Just as you once had feeding schedules and bedtime stories, you now have ways of connecting with your child that honor both their memory and your ongoing need to nurture and protect them. These might include lighting a candle on difficult days, wearing a piece of jewelry that reminds you of them, or setting aside time each week to sit quietly and talk to them about what is happening in your life.

Some parents find comfort in continuing birthday celebrations, creating new traditions that acknowledge their child's special day while adapting to the reality that they cannot be celebrated in traditional ways. Others find meaning in holiday rituals that include their child's memory, like hanging a special ornament or preparing their favorite food. These practices are not morbid or unhealthy; they are expressions of ongoing love and connection that serve the vital function of keeping your child present in your family's continuing story.

Parenting in absence also means making decisions with your child in mind, asking yourself what they would want you to do, how they would want to be remembered, what kind of life they would want you to live. This is not about living according to fantasy or projection, but about allowing your love for them to guide your choices in ways that honor both their memory and your own wellbeing. It might mean choosing to take better care of your health, to be more patient with your living children, or to pursue opportunities that feel aligned with the values you want to pass on in their name.

The physical objects that connect you to your child become sacred in ways that others might not understand. The shirt that still smells like them, their favorite blanket, a journal of their deepest thoughts, or the toy they never got to play with; these items are not just possessions but touchstones that allow you to feel close to your child when the distance between life and death feels unbearable. Keeping these objects close, touching them when you need comfort, sleeping with them when grief makes rest difficult, these are all valid expressions of your continuing love and your need to maintain physical connection in whatever ways remain possible.

Talking to your child becomes a natural part of your daily routine, as normal as the conversations you may once had when they were physically present. You might tell them about your day, share your fears, and hopes, ask for their guidance when you face complex decisions. These conversations are not signs of denial or inability to accept reality; they are expressions of a relationship that continues beyond death, a bond that remains active even though it can no longer be expressed through traditional means.

Photography takes on new meaning in parenting in absence. The pictures you have of your child become precious beyond measure, not just as memories but as proof of their existence, evidence of the love you shared, and windows into a relationship that others might not have had the chance to witness. You might find yourself talking to these photos, carrying them with you, or creating special displays that honor your child's place in your family. This is not living in the past; this is bringing the past into the present in ways that keep your child's love alive and active in your current life.

Parenting in absence often involves protecting your child's memory from a world that wants to forget, that is uncomfortable with ongoing grief, that believes healing means moving on rather than learning to carry love forward. You become the guardian of their story, the keeper of their memory, the one who ensures that their life continues to matter even though their physical presence has ended. This might mean correcting people who speak about your child in past tense, insisting that their name be included in family conversations, or creating opportunities for others to learn about who they were and what they meant to you.

This form of parenting requires tremendous courage because it means loving openly in a world that grows uneasy when grief does not follow a neat timeline or remain quietly contained. It means speaking about your child when others prefer silence, including them in family plans and conversations when others think you should move on, and maintaining rituals and traditions that keep them present when others believe such practices are unhealthy or excessive.

But parenting in absence is not just about maintaining connection with your child; it is also about allowing that connection to transform you in positive ways. Your child's love can inspire you to be more compassionate, more present, more aware of what truly matters. Their memory can guide you toward relationships and activities that align with your deepest values. Their spirit can give you strength to face challenges, comfort others who are struggling, and find meaning in experiences that might otherwise feel empty or pointless.

The goal of parenting in absence is not to keep your child alive in some literal sense, but to ensure that their love continues to flow through you into the world in ways that honor both their memory and your own continued existence. It is about creating a legacy that extends beyond their death, allowing their life to have ongoing impact through the choices you make, the kindness you show, and the love you share with others who need it.

This practice evolves over time, becoming more natural and less effortful as you learn what works for you and what feels authentic to your relationship with your child. What begins as desperate clinging to anything that reminds you of them gradually becomes a more peaceful and intentional way of keeping them close while also allowing yourself to engage fully with the life you must continue living.

Parenting in absence is ultimately about refusing to let death have the final word in your relationship with your child. It is about insisting that love is stronger than loss, that connection can transcend physical boundaries, and that being a parent is not just about the time you had together but about the lifetime of love you will carry forward in their honor.

Speaking Their Name

The defiant and healing act of speaking their name keeps your child's memory alive. It refuses to let their existence be erased by silence or others' discomfort. When you speak your child's name out loud, you declare that they lived, they mattered, and they are still loved.

You may notice others wince or change the subject, but saying their name is an act of love for your child and an act of self-respect for you as their parent. Michael's name is part of my vocabulary, as natural to say as the names of my living children. Making your child's name a normal part of your conversation claims their place in your family's ongoing story, ensuring their memory is never silenced.

Speaking your child's name is one of the most powerful ways to honor their life and maintain your connection with them. It is also one of the most challenging, because it requires you to navigate a world that is often uncomfortable with the ongoing presence of grief and prefers that the dead remain quietly in the past rather than actively remembered in the present.

The first time you say your child's name after they die, it might feel like you are summoning them back into the room with you. Their name on your lips becomes a bridge between the world where they lived and the world where they exist now, in memory and love and the space between heartbeats where the deepest connections are held. This is not imagination or wishful thinking; it is the real power of language to make the invisible visible, to bring love across the boundary between life and death.

But you will hastily discover that not everyone can handle hearing your child's name spoken aloud. Some people will physically recoil, their faces changing as if you have said something inappropriate or painful. Others will rush to change the subject, offering distractions or platitudes designed to move the conversation away from your child and back to safer ground. Still others will simply fall silent, unsure how to respond to the presence of grief in what they hoped would be a normal social interaction.

These reactions are not about you or your child. They are about other people's fear of loss, their discomfort with mortality, their inability to sit with pain that has no solution. They are about a culture that treats death as failure and grief as something to be overcome rather than integrated. They are about people who have not yet learned that love continues after death and that speaking about someone who has died is not morbid but necessary.

You cannot control these reactions, but you can decide how much power to give them. You can choose to let other people's discomfort silence you, or you can choose to speak your child's name anyway, understanding that their comfort is not more important than your need to honor your child's memory and maintain your role as their parent.

Speaking their name becomes a way of affirming their continued place in your life, even when the world around you does not know how to witness enduring grief. Every time you say their name in a conversation, you are insisting that they were real, that they mattered, that their life had significance that extends beyond their death. You are refusing to let silence erase their existence or minimize the impact they had on your life and the lives of others who loved them.

This practice requires courage because it makes your loss visible in ways that others might not expect or want. When you mention your child in casual conversation, when you include them in family stories, when you speak about them as naturally as you would speak about anyone else you love, you are challenging the assumption that death ends relationship and urges mourning to be tidy, contained, and quickly resolved.

But speaking their name also brings unexpected gifts. It keeps your child present in your daily life rather than locked away in a separate compartment labeled grief. It allows their personality, their quirks, their impact on your life to remain part of your story rather than becoming something you only think about in private moments. It gives other people permission to remember them too, to share their own memories if they have them, to acknowledge the ongoing reality of your love for them.

Sometimes speaking your child's name will bring comfort to others who are struggling with their own losses. When you mention your child in conversation, you might discover that someone else has experienced similar grief but has never felt safe talking about it. Your willingness to speak openly about your child can create space for others to share their own stories, leading to connections and conversations that would not have been possible if you had kept your grief private.

The practice of speaking their name evolves over time. In the beginning, it might feel forced or painful, like you are pushing words through a throat that wants to close. You might cry every time you say it or find that your voice breaks in ways that surprise you. This is normal and expected. Your body is learning to express love in a new way, and like any new skill, it takes practice to become natural and comfortable.

Eventually, saying your child's name becomes as natural as breathing. It stops feeling like an event and starts feeling like a normal part of conversation. You learn to gauge your audience and decide when and how to include your child in discussions, not because you are hiding or minimizing your grief, but because you are being strategic about where to invest your emotional energy and with whom to share your most precious memories.

You might develop different ways of speaking about your child depending on the context and the relationship. With close friends and family who knew them, you might share detailed stories and specific memories. With acquaintances or in professional settings, you might simply mention them in passing, making it clear that they are part of your family story without requiring a lengthy explanation or emotional response from others.

Speaking their name also means being prepared for questions that might be difficult to answer. People might ask how they died, how old they would be now, whether you have other children. Some of these questions come from genuine curiosity and care; others might feel intrusive or painful. You have the right to answer as much or as little as you choose, to redirect conversations that become too intense, and to protect your privacy while still honoring your child's memory.

The goal is not to make everyone comfortable with your child's name or to force others to engage with your grief in ways they cannot handle. The goal is to ensure that your child remains a living part of your vocabulary, your family story, and your ongoing life rather than becoming someone you only remember in private moments or on special occasions.

When you speak your child's name regularly and naturally, you are teaching the world that love does not end with death, that family includes those who are physically absent, and that grief is not something to be hidden but something to be honored. You are modeling a unique way of understanding loss, one that allows for ongoing connection and continuing bonds rather than insisting on closure and moving on.

Most importantly, speaking their name is a gift you give to your child and to yourself. It keeps them present in your daily life, allows their memory to be part of normal conversation, and ensures that their existence continues to have impact on the world through your willingness to make them visible to others. It is a practice that honors both your role as their parent and their ongoing place in your family, regardless of how others respond to their presence in your words and your heart.

Activating Enduring Love

You have arrived at one of grief's most sacred truths: death took your child's body, but it could never touch your love. That love is permanent, unshakeable, as real today as it was the moment your child drew their last breath. What has changed is not the love itself but how you express it, how you carry it, how you allow it to shape your continued existence in a world without your child's physical presence.

In the beginning, you may have believed that staying close to your child meant staying locked in pain, that moving forward would somehow betray or diminish the bond you shared. You may have watched yourself carefully, afraid that any moment of joy or peace would mean you were forgetting, abandoning, letting go. But you have learned that love and pain are not the same thing, even though pain can be evidence of love's depth.

Your love for your child does not require you to suffer. It does not demand that you remain frozen in the moment of their death. It asks instead that you carry them with you into everything that comes next; into your healing, into your transformation, into whatever meaning and purpose you choose to create from this loss.

You have begun to discover the difference between passive grief and active love. Passive grief keeps you stuck, waiting, unable to move because movement feels like leaving your child behind. Active love propels you forward, not away from your child but toward ways of honoring them that give their life ongoing impact in the world. It is the shift from preserving a memory like a photograph in a drawer to actively parenting in absence, making choices with your child in mind, speaking their name not as memorial but as living presence.

This chapter has shown you that continuing bonds are not just acceptable, they are essential. You do not need closure. You need connection. You do not need to move on. You need to move forward with your child woven into everything you do. The world may tell you to let go, but you are learning that holding on is not pathology. It is love refusing to be silenced by death.

Speaking your child's name becomes revolutionary. Every time you say it, you declare that they lived, they mattered, they are still loved. You refuse to let silence erase their existence. You push back against a culture that is uncomfortable with ongoing grief, that wants you to privatize your loss, that prefers dead children to remain unseen and unmentioned. Your child's name on your lips is resistance. It is witness. It is the audible form of love that refuses to die.

You have learned practical ways to activate this enduring love: creating rituals that maintain connection, wearing or carrying something that reminds you of your child, making daily choices that honor their memory, allowing their love to guide your decisions about how to spend your time and energy. These practices are not about denial or inability to accept reality. They are expressions of a relationship that continues beyond death, a bond that remains active even though it can no longer be expressed through traditional forms of physical care.

You are seeing and feeling that your child's love has transformed from something you received to something that flows through you. It shapes how you show up for others, how you respond to pain, yours, and others', how you understand what truly matters in life. Their love has made you more compassionate, more present, more willing to sit with the difficult truths that others want to avoid. This is their legacy, continuing to unfold through your choices and actions.

The beautiful truth at the heart of this chapter is that love does not end when breathing stops. It evolves. It adapts. It finds new channels and new expressions. Your love for your child is not a memory to be preserved in amber but a living force that continues to grow and change as you do. They are not frozen in the past; they are present with you now, in this moment, shaping who you are becoming.

Here are the specific actionable steps for activating your enduring love:

Create a small, private ritual to connect with your child daily, such as lighting a candle while you drink your morning coffee or speaking to their photograph before you go to sleep. Make this ritual simple enough that you can maintain it even on difficult days, understanding that consistency matters more than complexity. This daily practice keeps your child present in your routine rather than relegated to special occasions or moments of intense grief.

Choose one person you trust completely and make a point to say your child's name in conversation with them this week. Practice speaking about your child naturally, sharing a memory or mentioning them in the context of a family story. Notice how it feels to have their name in your mouth, to bring them into the present moment through words. This person becomes your practice ground for speaking openly about your child before you expand this practice to other relationships.

Identify a physical object that connects you to your child and place it somewhere you will see it every day, such as wearing a piece of jewelry, keeping a photo on your desk, or carrying something small in your pocket. This object becomes a tangible reminder of your ongoing connection, something you can touch when you need comfort or when you want to feel close to them throughout your daily activities.

When you feel a wave of love for your child, consciously think the words: I am carrying you with me. This simple phrase reinforces the idea that your love is not trapped in the past but is an active force in your present life. Say it out loud if you can, or whisper it silently, letting it remind you that your child's love continues to flow through you into everything you do.

Make one decision this week with your child in mind, asking yourself what they would want you to do or how you can honor their memory through your choice. This might be as simple as being extra kind to someone who is struggling, taking better care of your health, or choosing to engage in an activity that brings you joy rather than just going through the motions of daily life.

When someone changes the subject or seems uncomfortable after you mention your child, remind yourself that their discomfort is not your responsibility to manage. Your child's name deserves to be spoken, their life deserves to be remembered, and your love for them deserves to be expressed. Their reaction is about their limitations, not about your child's worth or your right to honor their memory.

Finally, identify one way you can let your child's love guide you toward helping someone else, whether through volunteering, supporting another grieving parent, or simply being more present and compassionate in your daily interactions. This transforms your grief into a gift you can offer to others, allowing your child's life to continue making a positive impact in the world through your actions and choices.

The love you have for your child is not something that existed in the past; it is a living force that exists right now, in this moment, guiding your breath and your heartbeat and your choice to keep living in their honor. This love is your child's legacy, your ongoing connection to them, and your pathway forward into a life that holds both grief and joy, both absence and presence, both the reality of death and the permanence of love.

Death took your child's body, but it could never touch the love between you. That love is yours to carry forward, to activate in service of their memory, and to use as a source of strength and guidance for whatever comes next in your journey of learning to live fully while honoring someone who cannot live alongside you in the traditional sense. You are not alone in this.

FINDING YOUR PEOPLE

Grief is an island you never chose to inhabit, and in the beginning, you are its only resident. The loneliness of that place cuts deeper than almost anything else because you find yourself speaking a language no one else seems to understand. People can visit your island, they can stand at the shoreline and call out words of comfort, but they cannot stay in this place where your child's absence fills every breath you take.

The isolation feels complete and permanent. You move through a world that continues spinning while you remain frozen in the moment everything changed. Friends and family members want to help, but their attempts often feel hollow because they have never walked this particular path. They offer platitudes about healing and time and your child being in a better place, not understanding that you do not want your child in a better place. You want them here, with you, where they belong.

The critical shift from isolating grief to shared understanding comes through finding your people. These are not the ones who try to fix you with well-meaning advice or fill the silence with uncomfortable chatter. These are the parents who speak the same language of loss, who know the ache that lives in your arms and the way anniversaries can feel like earthquakes that shake everything you thought you had rebuilt.

When you find them, or when they find you, something fundamentally changes. The air becomes easier to breathe. The weight you carry feels slightly less crushing because other hands help hold it. You discover that you can cry without apologizing and speak your child's name without watching someone wince. This community becomes your lifeline, the bridge between surviving your grief and learning to live with it in honor of your child.

The Critical Shift from Isolation

In the quietest moments after your child dies, you discover that loss has a way of making the world feel unbearably empty. The days stretch out like a thick fog where sound, light, and even your own breath feel muted and distant. You can be surrounded by people who love you deeply yet still feel utterly alone because no one else inhabits the same landscape of sorrow that has become your permanent address.

Grief pulls you out of the rhythm of normal life, leaving you standing still while everyone else keeps moving forward. They return to their jobs, their routines, their conversations about ordinary things that feel meaningless when measured against the weight of what you have lost. You watch them from behind a wall of pain that feels invisible to them but impermeable to you, wondering how the world can continue functioning when yours has stopped completely.

The isolation deepens because your grief makes others uncomfortable in ways they cannot name. Your raw pain reminds them of their own vulnerability, forcing them to confront the reality that terrible things can happen to good people without warning or reason. Some friends begin to avoid you, crossing the street when they see you coming or making excuses to skip gatherings where your presence might cast a shadow over their attempts at normalcy.

Others try to help but say things that cut like knives. They tell you that your child is in a better place, that everything happens for a reason, that you should be grateful for the time you had together. These words, meant to comfort, feel like betrayal because they ask you to find meaning in the meaningless, to accept the unacceptable, to be thankful for a love that was stolen from you far too soon.

You learn early that there is no going back to who you were before. Losing a child is not something you get over like a bad cold or recover from like a broken bone. It is something you learn to carry, and in those early years, carrying it alone feels impossible. The weight is too much for one person to bear, too heavy for a single heart to hold without breaking completely.

The person you were before your child died believed in safety nets and happy endings and the power of love to protect what mattered most. They thought they understood what loss meant because they had experienced disappointments and setbacks and the normal sorrows that are part of being human. They had no idea that real loss could reach inside you and rearrange every atom of your being, leaving you fundamentally changed at the cellular level.

That person is gone now, and in their place stands someone who knows too much about how quickly everything can change, how little control we really have over the things we love most. This new version of yourself moves through the world differently, with heightened awareness of suffering and a deep understanding that safety is an illusion that can be shattered in an instant.

Daily life transforms into unfamiliar terrain after your child dies. Ordinary tasks demand extraordinary effort, and familiar spaces can suddenly feel hostile. A song, a schoolyard, a checkout line, or a passing family can stop you in your tracks, reminding you of everything that has changed.

You may find yourself wondering how others continue so easily, unaware of how quickly life can fracture. The calendar itself becomes heavy, the birthdays, holidays, seasons, and milestones now carry both memory and grief, marking not just what was lost, but all that will now be remembered differently.

Even laughter feels like betrayal, as if experiencing joy means you are forgetting your child or minimizing the significance of your loss. In moments when laughter almost escapes you, shame can arrive just as quickly, insisting that joy is a betrayal, when in truth, your capacity to feel anything at all is evidence of your enduring love, not a failure of it. The spontaneous joy that once came easily now feels forbidden, another casualty of the loss that keeps taking things from you long after the initial death.

This isolation is not just emotional but physical. Your body remembers your child in ways that feel impossible to explain to others. Your arms ache with emptiness, your chest feels hollow, your muscles twitch with the phantom memory of holding someone who will never be held again. When I lost Michael, I woke up at feeding times to silence, my body still programmed for routines that no longer existed, producing milk for a baby who will never drink it.

The critical shift from isolation begins when you stop trying to make others understand your grief and start seeking out those who already do. This is not about giving up on the people who love you but cannot comprehend your pain. It is about recognizing that you need something they cannot provide, no matter how much they care about you or how desperately they want to help.

You need witnesses who have walked through the same fire, who know the specific weight of empty arms and the silence that fills a house where a child's laughter used to live. You need companions who understand that speaking your child's name is not dwelling on the past but keeping them present in your life. You need people who will not flinch when you cry without warning or try to cheer you up when sadness is the most appropriate response to your reality.

This shift requires tremendous courage because it means admitting that love alone is not enough to heal this kind of wound. The people who care about you most may not be the ones who can help you survive this darkness. It means venturing out of your protective cocoon of isolation to seek connection with strangers who share your unwanted membership in the club no one wants to join.

The first step is often the hardest: acknowledging that you cannot do this alone. Pride becomes a luxury you cannot afford when survival is at stake. The strength that carried you through other challenges in your life may not be sufficient for this one. You need help, and that help must come from people who understand the specific nature of your struggle because they have lived through it themselves.

When you begin searching for your people, you are not looking for answers, solutions, or ways to make the pain stop. You are looking for companionship in the darkness, for proof that others have walked this path and found ways to keep breathing, for evidence that the love you carry for your child can coexist with some form of continued life. You are seeking not healing but understanding, not recovery but community, not solutions but solidarity with others who know that some losses change you forever.

This search requires patience because your people may not appear immediately or in the places you expect to find them. They might be in support groups that meet in hospital conference rooms, homes, or community spaces. They might be in online forums where bereaved parents share their stories with strangers who become friends. They might be introduced to you by healthcare professionals who understand the importance of connecting grieving families with others who have survived similar losses.

The critical shift happens the moment you realize you are not the only person who has ever felt this particular kind of heartache. When you meet another parent whose eyes hold the same pain and experience yours do, when you hear someone speak about their child with the same mixture of love and longing that fills your own voice, when you discover that your experience, while unique in its details, is part of a larger human story of love that transcends death, the walls of isolation begin to crack.

This is not about finding people who will tell you that everything happens for a reason or that time heals all wounds. This is about finding people who will sit with you in the mess of your grief without trying to clean it up, who will listen to you talk about your child without suggesting that you need to move on, who will understand when you say that you are both devastated and grateful, both broken and somehow still breathing.

The shift from isolation to connection does not eliminate your pain or make your loss easier to bear. What it does is remind you that you are still human, still capable of relationship and understanding and the kind of deep connection that makes survival possible even in the darkest circumstances. It proves that love is stronger than death, not because death is defeated but because love finds ways to flow between hearts even when one of those hearts belongs to someone who is no longer physically present in the world.

The Gift of Shared Understanding

For me, what mattered most in those early days was not help in the way people usually mean it, but the quiet act of being witnessed. Penny, my Public Health Nurse, entered my home with attentiveness that asked nothing of me. She did not arrive to assess, advise, or guide me forward. She came willing to sit inside the reality of my loss, recognizing that grief had settled into every corner of my life, visible and invisible alike.

There was no expectation that I gather myself or explain what I was feeling. I did not need to make sense or be coherent. When words spilled out unevenly, she stayed. When all that came were tears or silence, she stayed then too. She did not try to make meaning of my pain or soften it with reassurance. Her presence did not lighten the loss, but it made space for it, and in that space, I did not have to carry it alone.

It was through being witnessed like this that I began to understand something essential: there are others who can stand beside this kind of grief without turning away. Parents whose bodies recognize the same ache, whose hearts understand the strange dissonance of loving a child who no longer breathes. At first, the idea of facing them may feel unbearable. To be seen by those who truly understand can make the loss feel sharper, more undeniable, when part of you is still protecting itself from the full weight of what has happened. That hesitation is not resistance; it is the slow, human process of learning how to exist in a world that has already been irrevocably changed.

The idea of walking into a room full of other bereaved parents can feel terrifying. You worry it will pull you back under, that their pain combined with yours will create a weight too heavy for anyone to survive. You fear that seeing their grief will intensify your own, that hearing their stories will make your loss feel even more permanent and impossible to bear.

There comes a point when the loneliness begins to feel more dangerous than the risk of being seen. Isolation may once feel like protection, but over time it starts to suffocate. For me, that shift did not happen quickly. It took seven years before I gathered the courage to attend my first SIDS conference. By then, I had learned how to appear functional in the world. How to show up, complete tasks, and keep moving. But beneath that surface, grief still dictated my inner landscape. It surged and dropped without warning, carrying fear, guilt, and sorrow that never truly rested.

I did not go because I felt prepared or strong. I went because continuing to live inside avoidance had become unbearable. I knew, deep down, that distancing myself from my grief was different from tending to it. Honoring Michael required more than endurance; it required presence. And I sensed that if I did not turn toward the pain I had been outrunning, it would continue to define my life from the shadows.

Walking into that space, my body reacted before my mind could catch up. My chest tightened, my breath shortened, and every instinct told me to retreat. Then I looked around and saw faces that felt achingly familiar. Parents whose eyes carried the same depth of loss, the same knowing that comes from surviving the unimaginable. There was no need for careful explanations or polite conversation. We recognized one another immediately. Our grief spoke for us.

Over the course of that gathering, something inside me loosened. Stories were shared, not only about death, but about life. About personalities, quirks, laughter, and the ways our children had reshaped us in the time we were given. We mourned together what would never come, and we also allowed space for moments of warmth that reminded us that our love had not disappeared. For the first time in a long while, grief felt shared rather than carried alone.

For the first time since Michael's death, his name rested in the air without hesitation or discomfort, spoken openly among people who understood that saying his name was an act of love, not something to be managed or avoided. I could talk about his first smile, his stubborn personality, the way he felt in my arms, without watching the listener's face change or feeling the conversation shift away from my child toward safer topics. These parents understood that our children were not just tragedies to be overcome but real people who deserved to be remembered and celebrated.

The gift of shared understanding is not that it makes your grief smaller or your loss more bearable. The gift is that it makes you feel less alone in carrying a weight that no one should have to carry at all. When another parent nods in recognition as you describe the physical ache in your arms, when someone else talks about the way holidays have become landmines, when you hear your own experience reflected in another person's words, you realize that your response to losing your child is not abnormal or excessive but entirely appropriate to the magnitude of your loss.

These connections teach you that grief has its own geography, its own language, its own customs that can only be understood by those who have citizenship in this unwanted country. Other bereaved parents know why you still set a place at the table for your child on their birthday. They understand why you keep their room exactly as it was. They do not question your need to talk about your child or suggest that you are stuck in the past when you share memories.

In this shared space of love and loss, you discover that you can remember your children for who they were, not just how they died. Your child becomes more than a tragic story; they become a whole person with quirks and preferences and a personality that made them uniquely themselves. Other parents help you hold onto these details, encouraging you to share the funny stories alongside the sad ones, to celebrate what was beautiful about your child's life even as you mourn what was lost.

The understanding flows in both ways. As you receive comfort from others who have walked this path, you also discover that your presence brings comfort to them. Your survival becomes proof that theirs is possible. Your willingness to speak about your child gives them permission to speak about theirs. Your tears validate their tears, and your love validates their love.

This mutual support creates a different kind of family, one bound not by blood but by shared experience of the deepest loss imaginable. These relationships often become some of the most important in your life because they are built on complete honesty about the hardest thing you have ever faced. There is no pretense, no need to protect others from the reality of your pain, no pressure to be anything other than exactly where you are in your grief journey.

Leaving that conference did not mean my grief had lifted. The ache of Michael's absence remained steady and undeniable. But I carried something different with me, an awareness that my love for him did not exist in isolation. There were others who could hold his memory with care, who understood when I needed words and when silence was enough. In that collective tenderness, I felt a subtle but meaningful shift: grief was no longer something I endured alone, but something I could live alongside, guided by love for my son.

The gift of shared understanding changes how you carry your grief because it reminds you that love this deep is not abnormal but sacred, that pain this profound is not pathological but appropriate, that the bond between parent and child is not broken by death but transformed by it. When you find your people, you find witnesses to your love, companions for your journey, and proof that even the darkest experiences of human life can be survived when we do not have to face them alone.

This understanding does not erase your pain, but it changes how you hold it. You are no longer walking alone in a world that cannot comprehend your loss. You are part of a community that knows exactly what you have lost and exactly how much it matters. In grief, that connection is everything.

Building Your Lifetime Community

Finding your people can grow into something much larger and more sustaining than temporary comfort during your darkest days. It can become the foundation for building a lifetime community that holds space for your ongoing grief while also supporting your continued growth and healing. This community becomes the place where you can stop softening the edges of your pain to make others comfortable and start living authentically as someone whose life has been forever changed by love and loss.

For me, this transformation began after that first SIDS conference when I realized I could not let go of the connection I had found with other bereaved parents. The relief of being understood, of speaking freely about Michael, of existing in a space where my grief was not seen as a problem to be solved but as love to be honored, was too precious to experience only during weekend gatherings or annual events.

I joined the Inland Empire Guild for Infant Survival, a community of SIDS parents whose strength had been forged in the fire of loss, but whose hearts remained committed to loving fiercely in the face of unimaginable pain. In our support group meetings, we held each other through tears and celebrated each other's steps forward, no matter how small they seemed to the outside world. We spoke openly about our babies, sharing their names, their personalities, the ways their memories still lit up our lives even in their physical absence.

We did not just share grief; we shared love. And in that sharing, we found a kind of healing that was only possible together, a recognition that our babies' lives had created bonds between us that extended far beyond the circumstances of their deaths. We became parents to each other's children in some ways, keepers of stories and memories, witnesses to lives that the world might otherwise forget.

Building a lifetime community means recognizing that your need for understanding and support does not end when the acute phase of grief passes. Years after your child dies, you will still have moments when the loss hits you with unexpected force. You will still need people who understand why anniversaries are difficult, why certain songs make you cry, why seeing other families living the life you were supposed to have can stop you in your tracks.

This community becomes a place where you can continue to parent your child through memory and ritual, where speaking their name is not just accepted but encouraged. In this circle of people who understand, you are not the person who lost a child or the family touched by tragedy. You are simply your child's parent, carrying them forward in the most natural way possible, through love that refuses to be silenced by death.

As my connection with this community deepened, my own grief began to grow roots in purpose. I trained with the California SIDS Program to become a peer support parent, someone who could stand beside newly bereaved families in those first unbearable days and weeks, just as

Penny and others had stood by me. I learned how to listen without rushing, how to hold space for the chaos of loss, how to offer my own story as proof that survival was possible even when it felt impossible.

This role taught me that carrying my child forward could take many forms. Sometimes it meant sitting in silence with a parent whose child had died just days before, letting them know through my presence that they were not alone in the darkest place they had ever been. Sometimes it meant sharing practical information about funeral arrangements or support services. Most often, it meant simply bearing witness to another parent's love and pain, validating their experience by reflecting it back to them through my own story of loss and loving forward without guilt or judgment.

Over time, my involvement in this community expanded in ways I never could have imagined when I first walked through those conference doors. I helped plan annual gatherings where parents could come together to learn, share, and honor their children. I spoke at events, not as an expert in research or policy but as an expert in love, the kind that survives death and continues to shape every choice you make.

I became an advocate at state and national levels, fighting for more funding for SIDS research, better support systems for bereaved families, and recognition that our babies' lives and deaths mattered in ways that extended far beyond our individual families. In every meeting, every conversation, every advocacy trip, Michael was with me. His name was on my lips, his love in my heart, his memory driving my commitment to ensuring that other families would have the support I had needed but did not always receive.

This work did not erase my pain, because nothing could do that. But it gave my pain a place to go, a way to be transformed into something that served other families walking the same brutal path. It became something I could pour into the world, turning grief into action, heartbreak into hope for others who needed to know that survival was possible.

Building a lifetime community also means learning to receive support as well as give it. There were times when I was the one who needed to be held up by others, when my own grief threatened to overwhelm me and I had to lean on the strength of parents who had been walking this path longer than I had. The community I had helped build became the net that caught me when I fell, the hands that pulled me back to my feet when I could not find the strength to stand alone.

This mutual support creates a different understanding of strength and vulnerability. In this community, admitting that you are struggling is not weakness but wisdom. Asking for help is not failure but recognition that some burdens are too heavy for one person to carry alone. Showing up for others when they need support is not obligation but privilege, a way of honoring your own child by ensuring that no parent must face this darkness without companions who understand.

The lifetime community you build may look different from mine. It might be centered around a specific type of loss, like stillbirth or childhood cancer or sudden infant death syndrome. It might be geographically based, bringing together bereaved families in your local area. It might be virtual, connecting you with parents around the world who share your experience through online forums and social media groups.

What matters is not the specific form your community takes but the function it serves and the space it delivers in your life. This community becomes the place where your child's life continues to matter, where their memory is kept alive through shared stories and ongoing love. It becomes the space where you can continue to grow and heal while never being asked to leave your grief behind or pretend that your loss was nothing less than devastating.

In this circle of people who understand, you discover that you can be both grieving and living, both broken and becoming, both forever changed by loss and still capable of joy and purpose and deep connection with others. You learn that your child's death, while it ended their physical presence in your life, does not have to be the end of their story or the end of yours.

Through the Guild, through my advocacy work, and through every parent I have met along the way, I have found my lifetime community. Together, we carry our children forward not in silence but openly, where their names are spoken, their stories shared, and their lives honored in ways that create ripples far beyond the years they were physically present with us.

This community becomes part of how you survive, not just the immediate crisis of loss but the lifetime work of learning to live fully while carrying someone you can never hold again. It reminds you that love is stronger than death, not because death is defeated but because love finds ways to continue flowing between hearts, creating connections that honor both what was lost and what remains.

Connecting With Other Bereaved Parents

You have walked through one of grief's loneliest territories and discovered that isolation is not inevitable. There are others who know this road, who speak the language of loss that cannot be taught, only learned through living it. This chapter shows you that while your grief is unique to your child and your bond with them, the landscape of bereaved parenthood is shared ground where genuine understanding becomes possible.

The loneliness of child loss is profound. Your grief makes the world uncomfortable. Friends fall silent, not knowing what to say. People disappear, unable to bear witness to pain they cannot fix. Even those who love you most may struggle to hold space for the depth and duration of your loss. You find yourself editing your words, hiding your tears, pretending to be better than you are, simply to make others comfortable. The isolation this creates can feel almost as devastating as the original loss.

But you have learned that there are parents whose eyes mirror your own. Who have survived the unsurvivable and can sit with you in the darkness without trying to turn on the lights. These are not people who happened to meet at a support group or online forum. They are witnesses who recognize each other instantly, who share a common language that requires no translation, who understand that speaking your child's name is not dwelling in the past but keeping them present.

You have discovered the gift of being truly seen. When another bereaved parent nods as you describe the ache in your arms, when someone else mentions the way holidays have become minefields, when you hear your own experience reflected in another person's words you realize that your response to losing your child is not abnormal or excessive but entirely appropriate to the magnitude of your loss.

These connections do not make your grief smaller. They do not take away the pain. But they do make you feel less alone in carrying a weight that no one should have to carry at all. There is profound relief in not having to explain, in not having to watch someone's face change when you mention your child, in not having to apologize for the duration or intensity of your grief.

You have learned that shared understanding flows both ways. As you receive comfort from others who have walked this path, you discover that your presence brings comfort to them. Your survival becomes proof that theirs is possible. Your willingness to speak about your child gives them permission to speak about theirs. Your tears validate their tears, and your love validates their love.

In this shared space, your child becomes more than a tragic story. They become a whole person with quirks and preferences and a personality that made them uniquely themselves. Other bereaved parents encourage you to share the funny stories alongside the sad ones, to celebrate what was beautiful about your child's life even as you mourn what was lost.

You are learning that finding your people is not about replacing the relationships you had before your loss. Many of those relationships may survive and even deepen through your grief. But you are building a different kind of family. One bound not by blood but by shared experience of the deepest loss imaginable. These relationships often become some of the most important in your life because they are built on complete honesty about the hardest thing you have ever faced.

The courage it takes to step into a room full of other bereaved parents, to attend a support group or conference, to join an online community. This courage is not something you manufactured. It comes from the same place as all courage after loss: from love for your child that refuses to let isolation define your life. You go not because you feel strong but because continuing to hide from your grief has become more dangerous than facing it.

You have discovered that these connections teach you your grief has its own customs, its own geography, its own culture that can only be understood by those who have citizenship in this unwanted country. Other bereaved parents know why you still set a place at the table for your child on their birthday. They understand why you keep their room exactly as it was. They do not question your need to talk about your child or suggest you are stuck when you share memories.

Finding your people changes how you carry your grief because it reminds you that love this deep is not abnormal but sacred, that pain this profound is not pathological but appropriate, that the bond between parent and child is not broken by death but transformed by it. When you find your witnesses, you find companions for your journey and proof that even the darkest experiences of human life can be survived when we do not have to face them alone.

Here are the specific actionable steps for connecting with those who know:

Search online for a support group specific to your type of loss, whether it focuses on SIDS or all other circumstances that took your child from you. Commit to attending one meeting, even if you participate virtually from the safety of your own home. You do not have to share your story or even speak at all; simply being present in a space where others understand your experience can begin to crack the walls of isolation that have surrounded you since your loss.

If you can, identify one person in your existing circle of family and friends who has proven they can sit with your pain without trying to fix it, someone who does not flinch when you cry or change the subject when you mention your child. Reach out to this person specifically when you need someone to witness your grief, understanding that while they may not have walked your exact path, they have demonstrated the capacity to hold space for your sorrow without making it about their own comfort.

When you feel ready, consider sharing a small part of your story in a safe, moderated online forum for bereaved parents. This might be as simple as posting your child's name and angel date or a short sentence about who they were to you. Notice how it feels to have their existence acknowledged by others who understand the magnitude of your love and loss, to receive responses from parents who honor your child's life without trying to minimize your pain.

Practice saying these words out loud: "I am looking for people who understand what it means to love a child I cannot hold." This phrase can help you identify and connect with others who share your experience while also reminding yourself that your search for community is not about finding people to fix your grief but about finding companions who can walk alongside you as you learn to carry it.

If attending in-person or online meetings feels too overwhelming, start by reading books written by other bereaved parents, listening to podcasts where they share their experiences, or enrolling in self-paced grief courses designed by a bereaved parent for bereaved parents. This allows you to hear stories like yours and begin to feel less alone in your grief while maintaining the privacy and control that early grief often requires. Let these voices remind you that others have survived losses like yours and found ways to honor their children while continuing to live.

When you encounter someone else who is newly bereaved, whether through support groups or chance meetings, remember that your survival is proof that theirs is possible. Your willingness to speak about your child gives them permission to speak about theirs. Your presence becomes a gift to them, just as the presence of others who have walked this path becomes a gift to you.

Finally, give yourself permission to need this community for the rest of your life, understanding that finding your people is not a temporary coping strategy but a permanent source of support and understanding. Your child's death created bonds between you and other bereaved parents that will continue to matter as you navigate anniversaries, holidays, and all the ongoing challenges of learning to live fully while carrying someone you can never hold again.

The profound isolation that follows child loss is not something you must endure forever. There are others who speak your language, who understand your love, who can sit with you in the darkness without trying to turn on lights you are not ready for. Finding your people is not about replacing the relationships you had before your loss but about adding connections that can hold the fullness of who you have become since your child died.

Your grief makes you part of a community you never wanted to join, but within that community, you can find understanding, support, and proof that love continues to flow between hearts even when one of those hearts belongs to someone who is no longer physically present in the world. In this shared space of love and loss, you discover that you are not alone, that your child's life continues to matter, and that the love between you can guide you toward connections and purpose you never could have imagined before loss taught you how strong that love really is. You are not alone in this.

FROM GRIEF TO PURPOSE

Pain that feels unbearable can become something else entirely when you learn how to pour it into the world with intention. This shift from surviving grief to transforming it into meaningful action does not happen quickly, it is not linear or follows a predictable timeline. For some parents, it begins within months of their loss. For others, like me, it takes years before the idea of purpose feels possible or even desirable.

Seven years passed before I found the courage to attend my first SIDS conference. Seven years of learning to function in the world while carrying Michael with me in ways that felt both sacred and insufficient. Seven years of wondering if there was something more, I could do with the love that had nowhere to go in traditional ways, something that could honor his life while giving my pain a place to be useful rather than only devastating.

That first conference became a turning point, not because it erased my grief but because it showed me how grief could become a bridge to others who needed what I had learned through surviving the unsurvivable. The work that grew from those few days did not make Michael's death meaningful or acceptable. Nothing could do that. But it gave his love a way to continue flowing into the world through my hands, my voice, my presence with families who were just beginning their own journey through unimaginable loss.

This transformation from grief to purpose is not about finding reasons for your child's death or discovering that everything happens for a plan you cannot see. It is about refusing to let their death be the end of their story, choosing instead to let their life continue having impact through the choices you make, the kindness you show, and the ways you use your sacred wisdom to help others who are walking the path you never wanted to know existed.

The Powerful Transformation of Pain

There comes a moment in your grief journey when you realize that the pain you carry can become something more than a weight that threatens to crush you. This realization does not arrive like a lightning bolt or a sudden revelation that changes everything at once. It creeps in slowly, quietly, during the small moments when you find yourself reaching out to another grieving parent or speaking words of comfort that you wish someone had said to you in your darkest days.

The transformation begins when you understand that your pain has taught you things about love, loss, and survival that cannot be learned any other way. You have walked through fire and emerged with knowledge that could help others who are just entering the flames. Your broken heart has developed a capacity for compassion that runs deeper than you ever imagined possible. Your experience of carrying impossible grief has given you strength you never knew you possessed.

This is not an attempt to reframe loss as meaningful or to suggest that your child's death was a necessary passage toward personal growth. Your child's death was not necessary for anything. It was a tragedy that stole a precious life and left a hole in the world that will never be filled. But the love that created your grief, the wisdom that emerged from your survival, the understanding you gained about what really matters, these can become gifts you offer to others who need them desperately.

The transformation happens when you stop asking why this happened to you and start asking how you can use what happened to you to help others who are facing similar darkness. When you shift from "Why did my child have to die?" to "How can my child's life and death make a difference for other families?" you begin to discover that purpose can emerge from the deepest pain without that pain becoming less significant or your child's death becoming acceptable.

For me, this shift began during that first SIDS conference when I met other parents whose children had died the same way Michael had. Their stories were different from mine in the details but identical in the depth of love and loss they carried. When I shared my experience of those early days, the isolation and confusion and desperate need for someone who understood, I saw recognition in their eyes that told me my words were landing in places that needed them.

One mother approached me afterward and said that hearing me talk about the physical ache in my arms had been the first time she felt understood in months of well-meaning but hollow comfort from friends and family. Another father thanked me for mentioning how ordinary tasks had become impossible, how making a cup of coffee could feel like climbing a mountain. These small moments of connection showed me that my experience, as painful as it had been, could become a source of healing for others.

The transformation of pain into purpose does not require grand gestures or life-changing career moves. Sometimes it looks like volunteering at a local hospital to hold babies in the NICU. Sometimes it means donating to research organizations working to prevent the kind of loss you experienced. Sometimes it involves nothing more than being the friend who knows what to say and what not to say when someone else faces tragedy.

Your transformed pain becomes a filter through which you see the world differently. You notice suffering that others might miss because you recognize the signs of someone who is barely holding on. You offer presence instead of solutions because you know that presence was what you needed most in your darkest moments. You speak honestly about loss and grief because you understand how much damage can be done by people who mean well but say all the wrong things.

This transformation also changes how you understand your role as your child's parent. You are no longer just someone who loved them while they were alive and now mourns them in their absence. You become someone who carries their love forward into the world in ways that create ripples of kindness, understanding, and support that extend far beyond your individual family. Your child's life begins to have impact through your choices, your actions, your willingness to turn your pain into a source of healing for others.

The powerful truth about transforming pain into purpose is that it does not diminish your grief or make your loss easier to bear. Your child is still gone. Your arms still ache for them. The life you planned together is still impossible. But alongside that permanent sorrow, you discover that your love for them can become an active force for good in the world, that their death does not have to be the end of their influence on the lives of others.

When I trained to become a peer support parent, I learned that my presence with newly bereaved families was not about having the right words or offering perfect comfort. It was about being living proof that survival was possible, that the love they felt for their child would not destroy them even though it felt like it might. My existence, my ability to speak their child's name without falling apart, my willingness to sit with them in their darkest moments, these became ways of honoring Michael while serving families who needed what I had learned through losing him.

The transformation requires you to believe that your child's life mattered enough to continue having impact through your choices and actions. It asks you to see their death not as the end of their story but as the beginning of a different chapter, one where their love flows through you into the world in ways that bring comfort, understanding, and hope to others who are walking the same impossible path.

This does not happen automatically or easily. There will be times when you feel too broken to help anyone else, when your own grief demands all your attention and energy. There will be moments when the idea of purpose feels meaningless in the face of what you have lost. These feelings are valid and necessary parts of your journey.

Transformation cannot be forced or rushed, and it cannot happen until you have done the essential work of learning to survive your own loss. But when you are ready, when the time feels right for reasons you cannot explain but can feel in your bones, you may discover that your pain has been quietly preparing you for something you never expected. Your grief has been teaching you about love that transcends death, about strength that emerges from brokenness, about the ways that one person's story of survival can become a lifeline for others who are drowning in their own sorrow.

The transformation of pain into purpose becomes one way of answering the question that haunts every bereaved parent: How do I live in a world where my child does not? Part of the answer is that you live in ways that honor their memory, that let their love continue to flow through your actions, that refuse to let their existence be forgotten or dismissed as insignificant. You live in ways that prove their life mattered by using what their death taught you to help others who need that knowledge desperately.

Carrying Your Child Forward

The active practice of carrying your child forward transforms your role from someone who once parented through physical presence to someone who parents through memory, intention, and the conscious choice to let their love guide your actions in the world. This is not about keeping them alive in some literal sense but about refusing to let death have the final word in your relationship with them.

Michael became the invisible thread that stitched my life back together after it had been torn apart by his death. He was there when I comforted another parent who lost their child, his memory giving me the words they needed to hear and the presence they needed to feel. He was there when I spoke at conferences, his name on my lips and his love in my heart as I shared our story with parents who needed to know that survival was possible.

He was there during every advocacy meeting where I fought for better support systems for bereaved families, every conversation where I pushed for more funding for SIDS research, every moment when I insisted that our babies' lives and deaths mattered in ways that extended far beyond our immediate families. In every meeting and conversation, his spirit guided my choices and gave meaning to work that might otherwise have felt overwhelming or impossible.

Carrying your child forward means making decisions with them in mind, asking yourself what they would want you to do, how they would want to be remembered, what kind of legacy they would want their life to create. This is not about projecting your own desires onto their memory but about letting your love for them inform your choices in ways that honor both their life and your continued existence in a world they can no longer inhabit physically.

Sometimes carrying them forward looks like taking better care of yourself because your body is the vessel that holds their memory and carries their love into the world. Sometimes it means being more patient with your living children because you understand how precious and fragile life really is. Sometimes it involves pursuing opportunities that feel aligned with values you want to pass on in their name, even when those opportunities require courage you are not sure you possess.

This practice also involves protecting their memory from a world that wants to forget, that is uncomfortable with ongoing grief, that believes healing means moving on rather than learning to carry love forward. You become the guardian of their story, the keeper of their memory, the one who ensures that their existence continues to matter even though their physical presence has ended.

When people suggest that you should stop talking about your child or that mentioning them makes others uncomfortable, carrying them forward means choosing to speak their name anyway. When society expects you to return to normal as if nothing has changed, carrying them forward means insisting that everything has changed and that this change includes beautiful things as well as devastating ones.

Your child becomes part of your vocabulary in the same way that your living children are part of your vocabulary. Their name flows naturally in conversation when the context feels right. Their preferences and personality traits become part of family stories. Their impact on your life gets woven into your narrative, explanations of who you are, and why you make the choices you make.

Carrying your child forward also means allowing their love to transform you in positive ways that you can offer to others. Your child's life taught you things about what really matters, about how precious each moment is, about the depth of love that is possible between human beings. These lessons become gifts you can share with others through your presence, your choices, your willingness to show up authentically in a world that often values surface over substance.

The love you carry for them becomes a source of compassion for others who are suffering, understanding for others who are struggling, patience for others who are learning. When you encounter someone who is going through a tough time, your child's love guides you toward responses that offer genuine comfort rather than empty platitudes, real presence rather than uncomfortable avoidance.

This carrying forward is not passive but active, requiring conscious choices about how to live in ways that honor their memory while also serving your own need to find meaning and purpose in your continued existence. It means looking for opportunities to let their love flow through your actions, whether that involves formal volunteer work or simply being more kind to strangers who are having difficult days.

Some parents carry their children forward through advocacy work, becoming voices for research, policy changes, or support systems that could prevent other families from experiencing similar losses. Others do it through creative expression, writing books, making art, or composing music that captures something essential about their child's spirit and impact. Still others carry them forward through acts of service that have no direct connection to the circumstances of their loss but reflect the values and love that their child brought into the world.

The key is finding ways that feel authentic to your relationship with your child and sustainable for your own wellbeing and healing. Carrying them forward should not become another burden you carry or another source of guilt when you cannot live up to impossible standards. It should feel like a natural extension of your love for them, a way of continuing the relationship that death interrupted but could not end.

When I trained to become a peer support parent, I was carrying Michael forward by using what his death had taught me to help other families who were just beginning their own journey through unimaginable loss. When I spoke at conferences or training, I was carrying him forward by ensuring that his story became part of a larger narrative about love that survives death and parents who refuse to let their children be forgotten.

When I advocated for better support systems and more research funding, I was carrying him forward by working to create a world where other families might have resources and understanding that I had needed but did not always receive. Every letter and email I wrote to legislators, every meeting I attended, every conversation I had with healthcare providers about the needs of bereaved families was a way of letting Michael's life continue to have impact on the world.

But carrying him forward also happened in smaller, more private ways. It happened when I chose to be more present with friends who were struggling because I understood how much presence had mattered during my own darkest days. It happened when I spoke honestly about grief and loss instead of pretending everything was fine because I knew how isolating it felt to carry pain that no one wanted to acknowledge.

It happened every time I made a decision based on what really mattered rather than what was expected or convenient, every time I chose connection over surface interaction, every time I offered comfort to someone who was suffering in ways that others might not notice or understand. These choices were guided by what Michael's love had taught me about the importance of showing up authentically for other human beings who are trying to navigate the complexities and sorrows of being alive in a world that can be both beautiful and devastating.

Carrying your child forward is ultimately about refusing to let their death be the end of their influence in the world. It is about insisting that love is stronger than death, not because death is defeated but because love finds ways to continue flowing through the choices and actions of those who remain. It is about letting their existence continue to matter through the ways it changed you, the wisdom it gave you, and the compassion it created in your heart for others who are walking similar paths of love and loss.

Building a Legacy in Their Name

Building a legacy means ensuring your child's life and death continue to matter in ways that extend far beyond the time they spent physically present in the world. This legacy can take countless forms, from public advocacy work to private family traditions, from formal organizations to simple acts of kindness that reflect the values you want to honor in their memory.

A legacy does not have to be grand or visible to be meaningful. It can be as public as national advocacy campaigns or as private as the way you choose to treat service workers with extra kindness because your child's death taught you how much small gestures of care can matter to someone who is struggling. It can mean planning annual conferences that bring bereaved families together for support and education, or it can mean simply being that friend who always supports others when they face tragedy.

The legacy you build in your child's name becomes one of the ways their life continues to create ripples of positive impact in a world that was blessed by their existence, however short that existence may have been. Every person who benefits from the work you do, the kindness you show, or the wisdom you share becomes part of your child's ongoing story, proof that their life had meaning that extends beyond their death.

For me, building a legacy in Michael's name began with my work as a peer support parent, but it expanded over time into roles I never could have imagined when I was first learning to survive his loss. I helped plan annual conferences where parents could come together to learn, share, and honor their babies in an environment where their ongoing grief was understood and supported rather than seen as pathological or excessive.

These gatherings became sacred spaces where parents could speak their babies' names freely, share memories that brought both tears and laughter, and connect with others who understood the specific challenges of learning to live after losing someone who meant everything to them. The conferences provided education about grief, resources for families, and opportunities for parents to support one another through the ongoing work of carrying their children forward.

I never set out to become someone who speaks about child loss. This path was carved by love and shaped by necessity. When Michael died, I was forced to learn how to survive in a world that no longer made sense, and everything I share now comes from that lived experience. I speak not because I have mastered grief, but because I continue to walk with it. My story of losing my son to SIDS, of learning to breathe again, of finding connection after isolation, is the offering I bring to other parents and to those who support them. I do not stand apart from this pain; I stand within it, reaching back with honesty and compassion, hoping my voice helps others feel less alone as they navigate their own impossible journeys.

The advocacy work that grew from these connections took Michael's legacy into legislative halls and research facilities, places where his name and story became part of larger conversations about supporting bereaved families and preventing future losses. I advocated at state and national levels for more funding for SIDS research, better training for healthcare providers who work with grieving families, and policies that recognized the ongoing needs of parents whose children had died.

In every meeting with legislators, every conversation with researchers, every letter to policymakers, Michael was present. His story became a human face on statistics, his death became evidence of the urgent need for better support systems, his life became proof that every baby matters regardless of how long they live. The work did not bring him back or make his death acceptable, but it ensured that his presence continued to have impact in ways that might help other families avoid similar losses or receive better support when losses occurred.

But building a legacy in your child's name does not require formal advocacy work or public speaking. It can happen through volunteering, donating to organizations that support families facing similar challenges, or creating scholarship funds that help other children access opportunities your child will never have. It can mean mentoring other bereaved parents, writing letters to families who have experienced recent losses, or simply living in ways that reflect the values your child's love taught you about what really matters.

Some parents build legacies through creative expression, authoring books or creating art that captures something essential about their child's spirit and impact. Others establish foundations or organize fundraising events that support research or provide direct assistance to families in need. Still others build legacies through the way they parent their living children, treating each day as precious because they understand how swiftly everything can change.

The legacy can also be built through the relationships you nurture and the community you help create around shared experiences of love and loss. Through my work with the Guild and my connections with other bereaved parents, I became part of a network of people who carry each other's children in their hearts, who remember birthdays and anniversaries, who show up for each other during the hardest moments and celebrate together during times of growth and healing.

This community became part of Michael's legacy because it was built on the foundation of what his death taught me about the importance of not walking through darkness alone. Every parent who found support through these connections, every family who felt less isolated because of the community we built together, every child whose memory was honored alongside Michael's became part of the ongoing impact of his brief but significant life.

Building a legacy also means teaching others about your child, sharing stories that help people understand who they were beyond the circumstances of their death. When I talk about Michael's stubborn personality, his first smile, the way he felt in my arms during that precious times we had together, I am building a legacy that honors his individuality and helps others see him as a whole person rather than just a tragedy.

These stories become gifts I can offer to others, proof that lives matter regardless of their length, evidence that love creates bonds that death cannot break. When other parents hear me talk about Michael with both sorrow and joy, they receive permission to remember their own children in complex ways that include celebration alongside grief, gratitude mixed with longing, pride in who their child was alongside anger about what was taken from them.

The legacy you build in your child's name becomes a bridge between the world where they lived and the world where they exist now, in memory and love and the ongoing impact of their existence in your life. It ensures that their story does not end with their death but continues through the choices you make, the kindness you show, the ways you use what their life and death taught you to make the world a little better for others who are walking similar paths.

Through the Guild, through my advocacy work, and through every parent I have met along the way, I have found ways to ensure that Michael's beautiful life leaves an imprint far beyond the years he was physically here. Together with other bereaved parents, we carry our children forward not in silence but in the open, where their names are spoken and their stories are shared, where their lives are honored and their deaths acknowledged as losses that matter deeply to the world they left behind.

This is how you make sure their presence continues to change the world: by refusing to let death have the final word, by insisting that love is stronger than loss, by building legacies that prove their lives had meaning that extends far beyond the time they spent in your arms. The legacy becomes part of how their love continues to flow through the world, creating connections and healing and hope in places where darkness might otherwise prevail.

Transforming Grief Into Purpose

You have reached territory that once seemed impossible: the place where grief begins to transform into something beyond survival, beyond endurance, beyond simply getting through each day. This is not about your pain disappearing or your loss becoming bearable. It is about discovering that your child's death, while it destroyed the life you planned, has also opened paths you never imagined. Paths toward meaning, toward service, toward a kind of purpose that can only be forged in the fire of profound loss.

Purpose after child loss is not something that arrives fully formed. It does not announce itself with clarity or certainty. For many bereaved parents, it begins as the smallest impulse to make something of this devastation, to ensure their child's life, no matter how brief, continues to create ripples in the world. It starts as a whisper: What if this pain could be transformed? What if my child's death could somehow lead to something that helps others?

You have learned that purpose is not about finding silver linings or believing that everything happens for a reason. You do not need your child's death to mean something in order to create meaning from it. This is a crucial distinction. Meaning making is active, intentional, chosen, not something imposed by fate or divine plan but something you construct from the raw materials of your experience.

The ways purpose manifests are as varied as the children who inspire it. For some parents, it looks like advocacy; working to change laws, improve safety standards, or raise awareness about the conditions that took their child. For others, it is direct service supporting newly bereaved parents, volunteering with organizations that serve families in crisis, or creating resources that did not exist when they needed them. For some, it is creative expression like writing, art, music that gives voice to grief and honors their child's memory.

Purpose can also be quieter, more personal. It might look like being more present with your living children, more compassionate with strangers, more willing to sit with others in their pain because you know what it means to be truly seen in your darkest hour. It might mean choosing work that aligns with your values, relationships that honor your whole story, or a life that prioritizes what truly matters over what merely appears important.

You have discovered that purpose does not require grand gestures or public platforms. It can be as simple as saying your child's name to keep their memory alive, as intimate as lighting a candle each morning in their honor, as revolutionary as refusing to let grief be hidden away like something shameful. Every choice you make to live differently because of your loss is an act of meaning-making.

This chapter has shown you that grief and purpose are not sequential. First you grieve, then you find purpose. They are intertwined, concurrent, sometimes indistinguishable from each other. Your grief fuels your purpose, and your purpose holds your grief. The pain never stops, but it begins to power something beyond itself.

You are learning that purpose often emerges not from asking "why did this happen?" but from asking "what now?" Not "what does this mean?" but "what meaning can I create?" The shift from passive victim of circumstance to active agent in your own narrative is subtle but powerful. You cannot control what happened to your child. But you can control what you do with your continued existence, how you honor their memory, what legacy you build from the love that refuses to die.

Many bereaved parents discover that their grief gives them access to a kind of radical empathy. The ability to meet others in their darkest places without flinching, to witness pain without trying to fix it, to offer presence without platitudes. This becomes purpose: using your hard-won wisdom to light the way for others stumbling through darkness you remember all too well.

You have learned that finding purpose does not mean you are "over" your grief or that you have somehow successfully "moved on." Your child's absence is still permanent. Your grief is still present. But you are discovering that you can be both devastated and purposeful, both shattered and useful, both eternally bereaved and meaningfully engaged with life.

The transformation from grief to purpose is not about becoming grateful for your loss. It is about refusing to let your loss be the only thing that defines you. It is about honoring your child by living in ways that reflect the love they awakened in you, the changes they created in you, the capacity for depth and compassion that your grief has carved out.

Here are the specific actionable steps for channeling love into action:

Identify one small act you can do this month to honor your child's memory in a way that helps others. This might be donating a book about grief to your local library in their name, volunteering at a children's hospital, or writing a letter of support to another bereaved family. Start with something manageable that feels meaningful to you, understanding that purpose often begins with small actions that grow over time into larger commitments.

Share one positive memory of your child with someone who did not know them, focusing on who they were rather than how they died. Tell a coworker about their personality, share a story with a friend, or post a photo with a caption about what made them special. This storytelling becomes a form of legacy building, ensuring that their existence is known and remembered by people beyond your immediate family.

Research one organization that works on issues related to your child's death or that supports families facing similar challenges. This might be a research foundation, a support organization, or a hospital program. Learn about their work and consider how you might support them when you feel ready, whether through donations, volunteering, or simply spread awareness about their mission. This research helps you understand how your child's story fits into larger efforts to help other families.

Write down what you want the world to know about your child, creating a brief but complete picture of who they were and what they meant to you. Include their personality traits, their impact on your life, and the ways their love continues to guide your choices. This written legacy becomes the foundation for future advocacy, storytelling, or simply your own remembrance of what made them uniquely themselves.

When you feel overwhelmed by the idea of purpose or legacy, remind yourself that carrying your child forward can be as simple as making one decision with them in mind. Ask yourself what they would want you to do in a specific situation, how they would want you to treat someone who is struggling, what kind of person they would want you to become. Let their love guide your choice, understanding that this guidance is one way you continue to parent even in their absence.

Connect with one other bereaved parent, either through support groups or online communities, and offer to listen to their story without trying to fix their pain. Your presence and understanding become gifts you can offer based on what you learned during your own darkest days. This connection honors your child by using your experience to help someone else feel less alone in their grief.

Finally, give yourself permission to find purpose gradually and in your own timing, understanding that transformation cannot be forced or rushed. Some days you will feel too broken to help anyone else, and that is perfectly normal and acceptable. Purpose emerges naturally from love when you are ready to channel it, not according to external timelines or expectations about when you should be doing meaningful work in your child's memory.

The transformation from grief to purpose is not about replacing your sorrow with action or finding ways to make your loss worthwhile. It is about discovering that your love for your child is so strong and permanent that it can become a source of healing for others while continuing to be the driving force in your own life. Your child's existence created love powerful enough to survive death and wise enough to guide you toward ways of living that honor both their memory and your own continued existence in a world they cannot share with you physically.

When you sit with others who understand, or when you offer even a small kindness shaped by your child's life, you are living the heart of After the Goodbye. You are holding love by letting their name and story move between you. You are releasing guilt by allowing yourself to receive support instead of carrying everything alone. You are loving forward each time their love guides how you show up in the world now; quietly, steadily, in ways that say, "Their life still matters, and so does mine."

This channeling of love into action becomes one of the most beautiful ways to carry your child forward, proving that their life had meaning that extends beyond their death, that their love continues to flow through your choices and actions, and that death cannot have the final word in a relationship built on bonds this deep and permanent. Through purpose born from pain, their beautiful life leaves ripples of good that spread far beyond the years they were here, touching lives they never met through the love that continues to guide everything you do in their honor. You are not alone in this.

WE SURVIVE BECAUSE THE LOVE NEVER DIES

When I first held this truth in my hands, it felt too fragile to trust, like morning light filtering through tears that might disappear if I looked at it too directly. The idea that we survive not because grief fades but because love endures seemed impossible during those early days when breathing itself felt like an act of rebellion against a world that no longer included Michael. How could love be enough when love was exactly what made the absence so unbearable?

But now, years into this journey of learning to live while carrying someone I cannot hold, I understand that this truth is not fragile at all. It is the strongest thing I know. The love that created my grief is the same love that carries me through each day, that guides my choices, that transforms my pain into something that can serve others who are walking the same impossible path. We survive because the love never dies, and that love becomes our compass, our strength, and our bridge between the world where our children lived and the world where we must continue living without their physical presence.

This final understanding brings together everything we have learned about surviving child loss. Your grief is not evidence of weakness or incomplete healing; it is proof of a love so deep that death cannot touch it. Your child's absence will always be felt, but their presence can be felt too, in new ways that honor both what was lost and what remains. The work of growing around grief while carrying your child forward is not about finding closure but about discovering that love creates its own form of forever, one that no ending can destroy.

Your Grief is the Evidence of Your Love

Society tells you that healthy people get over their losses, that time heals all wounds, that moving on is the natural progression from tragedy to recovery. These messages come from a world that fundamentally misunderstands what grief actually is, treating it like an injury that should close rather than recognizing it as love that has nowhere to go in traditional ways. Your grief is not a sign that something is wrong with you; it is proof that something was incredibly right between you and your child.

The depth of your sorrow matches exactly the depth of your love. When people suggest that your grief is too intense or lasting too long, they are unknowingly suggesting that your love was too intense or should not last so long. But you know instinctively that this is impossible. Your love for your child is not something that should diminish with time any more than your love for your living children should fade because years have passed since their birth.

Every tear you cry is a drop of liquid love with nowhere to go except down your cheeks. Every ache in your arms is your body remembering the weight and warmth of someone who belonged there. Every moment when their absence hits you like a physical blow is your heart insisting that they mattered, that they were real, that the bond between you cannot be severed by something as final as death.

Your grief is sacred because it is the external expression of an internal love that refuses to be contained by the boundaries of life and death. When you understand this, you can stop apologizing for your sorrow and start honoring it as the most beautiful tribute you can offer to your child. Your tears are not weakness; they are worship. Your longing is not pathology; it is devotion.

These reframing transforms everything about how you carry your grief. Instead of seeing it as something to overcome, you can embrace it as something to carry with pride. Your grief announces to the world that this child was loved completely that their life had immeasurable value, that their absence creates a void nothing else can fill because nothing else should fill it.

When someone tells you that you should be feeling better by now, you can respond with confidence that your grief is exactly the right size for the love that created it. When people suggest that dwelling on your loss is unhealthy, you can explain that you are not dwelling on loss but celebrating love, not stuck in the past but carrying the past forward into a future that includes your child in ways they cannot see but you can feel.

The evidence of your love shows up in countless ways throughout your days. It appears when you automatically reach for your phone to call them before remembering they cannot answer. It surfaces when you see something beautiful and wish you could share it with them. It emerges when you make decisions based on what they would want you to do, letting their love guide your choices even though they cannot speak the words aloud.

Your grief also serves as evidence for your child that they were loved beyond measure. If love continues after death, if connection transcends physical presence, then your child knows that your sorrow is proof of your devotion. Your tears tell them that they mattered, that they were wanted, that their spirit created an impact so profound that you will carry it for the rest of your life.

This understanding allows you to grieve without shame, to cry without apology, to speak your child's name with the same natural ease you would use for any other family member. Your grief becomes not something you hide but something you honor, not a burden you carry in secret but a badge of love you wear with dignity.

When people ask how you are doing, you can answer honestly that you are grieving and that this is exactly as it should be. When they express concern about your ongoing sorrow, you can reassure them that your grief is not a problem to be solved but a love to be celebrated. When they wonder when you will get over your loss, you can explain that you will never get over loving your child, and your grief is simply that love in a different form.

The world needs to understand that bereaved parents are not broken people who need fixing but loving people who are expressing that love in the only ways available to them now. Your grief teaches others about the power of human connection, the depth of parental love, and the ways that bonds can survive even the most devastating losses. Your willingness to grieve openly gives others permission to love deeply, knowing that such love comes with risks but also with rewards that make those risks worthwhile.

Years after Michael's death, I still cry when I think about his first smile, when I imagine the man, he might have become, when I wish I could hold him just one more time. These tears do not mean I am stuck, broken, or failing to heal properly.

They mean I am still his mother, still connected to him by love that death could not destroy, still honoring the bond we shared during his short but precious life. My grief has become my gift to him, my way of telling him every day that he was loved, that he mattered, that his existence changed everything about who I am and how I move through the world. When I cry for him, I am loving him. When I ache for him, I am remembering him. When I carry his memory into everything I do, I am parenting him in the only ways available to me now.

Your grief is not your enemy. It is your love made visible, your connection made manifest, your child's ongoing presence in your life taking the form it must take now that they exist in memory and spirit rather than in physical reality. This grief will never leave you, and that is not a curse but a blessing. It is proof that some loves are so strong that not even death can diminish them, so deep that they become part of who you are forever.

Carrying Your Child Into a Meaningful Future

The future stretches ahead of you like an endless road you never wanted to walk, especially not without your child beside you to share whatever comes next. In the beginning, the idea of a future without them feels not just impossible but wrong, like betraying their memory by continuing to exist in a world they cannot experience. But as you learn to grow around your grief while carrying their love forward, you discover that the future can become something different than what you planned but still meaningful in ways you never expected.

This meaningful future is not about replacing what you lost or finding adequate substitutes for the life you were supposed to share with your child. Nothing can replace them, and nothing should. The meaningful future you create is one that includes them in every important way except physical presence, one that honors their memory while also honoring your own need to continue living and growing and contributing to the world they can no longer inhabit directly.

Your child becomes your invisible companion on this journey into whatever comes next. They are present in your decision-making process, influencing your choices through the love they gave you and the wisdom their life taught you about what really matters. They guide you toward relationships that honor your whole story, including your identity as their parent. They inspire you to pursue opportunities that align with values you want to carry forward in their name.

The meaningful future includes speaking their name in conversations where their memory brings comfort or connection. It involves creating traditions that acknowledge their ongoing place in your family, even though they cannot participate in those traditions in traditional ways. It means making space for both joy and sorrow, understanding that a life lived in their honor can include laughter without betraying their memory, can embrace beauty without forgetting what was lost.

This future is built on the foundation of active love rather than passive grief. Instead of being paralyzed by what ended, you become energized by what continues. Your child's love flows through your actions, your choices, your responses to others who are struggling. Their existence becomes a source of strength that helps you face challenges, comfort that sustains you through difficulties, and wisdom that guides you toward what has lasting value versus what is merely temporary distraction.

Carrying your child into a meaningful future also means becoming someone they would be proud to call their parent. This is not about perfection or living according to impossible standards but about letting their love inspire you to be more compassionate, more present, more aware of the preciousness of every moment and every connection. Their death taught you things about life that you could not have learned any other way, and those lessons become gifts you can offer to others who need them.

The future you create in their honor might include advocacy work that helps other families facing similar challenges. It might involve volunteering with organizations that support children or bereaved parents. It might mean pursuing creative expression that captures something essential about their spirit and impact on your life. Or it might look like nothing more dramatic than being the friend who always knows what to say when someone else faces tragedy, the coworker who notices when someone is struggling, the family member who creates space for difficult emotions rather than rushing to fix them.

Your meaningful future includes the ongoing practice of parenting in absence, continuing to love and protect and guide your child in whatever ways remain possible. You parent them by keeping their memory alive, by sharing their story with others who need to hear it, by making choices that honor the values their love taught you. You parent them by refusing to let the world forget that they existed, that they mattered, that their life had significance that extends far beyond their death.

This future also acknowledges that your child's absence will always be felt alongside their presence. There will be graduations they cannot attend, holidays they cannot celebrate, milestones they cannot reach. These ongoing losses deserve recognition and grief, but they do not negate the meaningful ways their love continues to shape your life and the lives of others who are touched by your story.

The beautiful truth about carrying your child into a meaningful future is that it proves love is stronger than death, not because death is defeated but because love finds ways to transcend physical boundaries and continue flowing through the choices and actions of those who remain. Your child's influence on your life does not end with their death; it transforms and deepens and becomes part of everything you do from that moment forward.

This meaningful future becomes your gift to them, your way of ensuring that their short life continues to have impact in the world through your willingness to carry their love forward into whatever comes next. It is your promise to them that death will not have the final word in your relationship, that their existence will continue to matter through the ways it changed you and continues to guide you toward lives and choices that honor their memory.

When people ask about your plans for the future, you can speak with confidence about goals and dreams that include your child as an invisible but essential presence. When they wonder how you find meaning after such devastating loss, you can explain that meaning comes not from forgetting what happened but from refusing to let what happened be the end of the story. Your child's love gives your future purpose, direction, and the kind of depth that can only come from understanding what really matters when everything else falls away.

The road ahead is still long and sometimes difficult, but it is no longer empty. Your child walks beside you in spirit, their love lighting the way forward, their memory giving meaning to every step you take toward whatever beautiful and meaningful future you can create together. You will always be their parent, carrying them forward in ways love can.

Living With Continuing Bonds

You have arrived at a truth that is both simple and profound, both devastatingly sad and unexpectedly hopeful: the reason you survive the death of your child is not because the grief fades or the pain lessens or time heals what has been broken. You survive because your love for them is stronger than their absence. That love sustains you when nothing else can. It carries you through the darkest nights. It gives you reason to open your eyes to another morning. We survive because the love never dies.

This final chapter has woven together everything you have learned on this journey; from the first moments of shock through the shattering of identity, from the discovery that grief does not shrink through the courage it takes to find your people, from the smallest victories of early survival through the possibility of purpose emerging from devastation. All of it has been leading to this central understanding: love is the thread that connects every part of your experience, the foundation on which you rebuild, the force that propels you forward even when forward feels impossible.

You have learned that continuing bonds are not a stage to pass through or a phase to outgrow. They are the way you live now. Your relationship with your child has not ended; it has transformed. You are still their parent, even though you can no longer parent them in traditional ways. Your love for them is still active, still growing, still shaping your choices and priorities. They are still part of your family, your story, your daily life, not as memory preserved in amber but as presence woven through everything you do.

The fear that haunted you in the beginning, that you might forget them, that the world might forget them, that their life might be reduced to a date on a tombstone, this fear has been answered by your fierce commitment to keeping them present. You speak their name. You share their story. You make choices with them in mind. You honor their memory not just on special occasions but in the ordinary moments that make up a life. They are here, in your heart and in your hands, in your breath and in your purpose.

You have discovered that grief and joy are not opposites but companions. You can carry profound sorrow for what was lost while also experiencing moments of genuine happiness. You can ache with longing for your child while also appreciating the beauty that still exists in the world. You can honor their memory while also building a life that holds meaning and connection. Your grief does not diminish your joy; your joy does not betray your grief. Both are true. Both are real. Both are part of loving someone you cannot see or touch or hold.

This chapter has shown you that survival looks different than you thought it would. It is not about returning to who you were before or achieving some imagined finish line called "healed." It is about learning to carry your child with you always, to integrate their absence into your identity without being destroyed by it, to hold space for both the life that was lost and the life you choose to keep living in their honor.

You have learned that love does not require your child's physical presence to remain real. It does not need their body to continue growing and evolving. Your love for them is not trapped in the past; it is alive in you right now, in this moment, guiding your breath and your heartbeat and your choice to keep living even when living is hard.

The title of this book *After the Goodbye* has revealed its full meaning. There is an "after" to the moment your child died, an after to the initial shock, an after to the darkest days of early grief. But the goodbye is not final. You said goodbye to their body, to their physical presence in your life, to the future you planned together. But you did not say goodbye to your love for them. You will never say goodbye to that love. It is the constant, the anchor, the force that carries you through every after that comes.

We survive not because we are strong, though strength emerges from this survival. We survive not because time heals, though time changes how we carry our grief. We survive not because we have no choice, though choice often feels absent in the deepest pain. We survive because the love we have for our children is more powerful than death, more enduring than grief, more permanent than any loss we can experience. That love refuses to die. That love insists we keep breathing. That love writes the story of our continued existence even when we cannot see the words.

This is the final lesson and the first lesson: Love never dies. Everything else flows from this truth.

THE WAY FORWARD:
A SUMMARY OF ACTIONABLE LOVE

You have walked through the entire landscape of grief, from the first moments of world-shattering loss through the slow, painful work of learning to carry your child with you into whatever comes next. This final chapter distills everything you have learned into a framework you can return to again and again: the practices of holding love, releasing guilt, and loving forward.

Holding love is the practice of keeping your child present in your life. It is saying their name, sharing their story, creating rituals that honor their memory, making choices with them in mind. It is refusing to let their death erase their existence, refusing to let silence replace the sound of their name, refusing to let the world forget they were here. Holding love is active, intentional, defiant with a daily commitment to parenting in absence, to maintaining bonds that death cannot break.

Releasing guilt is the practice of letting go of the weight that does not belong to you. It is forgiving yourself for being human, for not being able to prevent what happened, for the moments you have felt joy or peace or hope in the midst of grief. It is understanding that surviving your child's death is not betrayal. That smiling does not mean you have forgotten. That building a life that holds meaning does not dishonor their memory. Releasing guilt is gentle, gradual, ongoing, a daily choice to be as compassionate with yourself as you would be with another bereaved parent.

Loving forward is the practice of allowing your love for your child to propel you into continued living. It is making meaning from your loss, finding purpose in your pain, using your grief as fuel for transformation. It is honoring your child by living in ways that reflect the love they awakened in you, by being present with others in their darkness, by refusing to let their death be the only thing that defines you or them.

Loving forward is courageous, creative, and chosen. It is a daily commitment to building a life that carries your child with you while also embracing the fullness of your own continued existence.

These three practices of holding love, releasing guilt, loving forward are not linear stages but concurrent activities, woven together, supporting each other, creating a framework for living after loss. Some days, holding love will feel most important. Other days, releasing guilt will require all your energy. Still other days, loving forward will call to you, inviting you to step into new possibilities. All three are always available. All three are always necessary.

You have learned that the way forward is not a straight path but a spiral, returning again and again to the same terrain from different perspectives, revisiting the same lessons at deeper levels, discovering new dimensions of truths you thought you already understood. Grief is not something you graduate from or complete. It is something you learn to carry with more skill, more grace, more intention over time.

This journey has taught you that there is no timeline for grief, no schedule your heart must follow, no deadline by which you must achieve acceptance or peace or healing. You move at the pace your grief demands, honoring your process without comparison to others, trusting that you are doing the work even when it does not feel like progress, knowing that survival itself is victory.

You have learned that community matters. That finding your people, speaking your truth, allowing yourself to be witnessed in your pain, are not luxuries but necessities for surviving child loss. You have discovered that your grief makes you uniquely qualified to meet others in their darkness, that your survival offers hope to those just beginning this journey, that your willingness to speak your child's name gives others permission to speak theirs.

The actionable steps throughout this book are not a program to complete or a curriculum to master. They are invitations to practice, to experiment, to discover what works for your unique grief and your unique child. Some will resonate immediately. Others will feel impossible right now but may become accessible later. All of them are offerings, not obligations, tools for your journey, not rules for right grieving.

As you move forward from here, remember there is no end to grief, but there is transformation. There is no closure, but there is continuing connection. There is no going back to who you were before, but there is becoming someone new. Someone shaped by love that transcends death, by knowledge earned through surviving the unsurvivable, by a capacity for depth and compassion that can only be forged in the fire of profound loss.

Your child's life matters. Your love for them matters. Your survival matters. The meaning you create from this loss matters. You matter, not despite your grief but with it, not after you heal but as you carry your loss, not when you reach some imagined finish line but right now, in this moment, as you practice holding love, releasing guilt, and loving forward.

This is the way forward. Not away from your child, but with them. Not past your grief, but through it. Not to a place where the pain disappears, but to a life large enough to hold both your loss and your love, both your sorrow and your strength, both who you were before and who you are becoming.

The love never dies. And because it never dies, neither do you. You keep breathing, keep living, keep loving, not because it is easy, but because that love asks nothing less of you. This is how we survive. This is how we honor them. This is how we live after the goodbye.

Your path forward is paved with active love, built from the understanding that survival comes not from letting go but from learning to hold on in a new way. The journey through child loss is not about healing in any traditional sense but about discovering how to carry your child with you always while creating a life that honors both their memory and your own continued existence in a world they cannot share with you physically.

The way forward begins with the most basic act of survival: focusing on your next breath when the weight of loss threatens to crush you completely. In those early moments, days, and weeks, your only task is to breathe, understanding that each breath you take is an act of love for your child, proof that their existence mattered enough to keep you fighting for your own continued life even when living feels impossible.

First, survive the moment by shrinking your world down to the size of a single breath, a single heartbeat, a single second of existence when the future feels unbearable and the past feels too painful to remember. Your energy is precious now, more precious than it has ever been, and you must guard it carefully, spending it only on what serves your survival and your connection to your child.

Second, honor your whole loss, including the loss of the person you were before your child died. Grieve not only for your child but for the parent you used to be, the future you had planned together, the innocence and certainty that died alongside them. This grief for your former self is not selfish but necessary, part of understanding the full scope of what was taken from you and what must be rebuilt from the pieces that remain.

Third, practice parenting in absence through small, daily rituals that keep your child present in your life rather than relegated to special occasions or moments of intense grief. Light a candle while you tell them about your day. Wear something that reminds you of them during family gatherings. Make decisions with them in mind, asking what they would want you to do, how they would want to be remembered, what kind of person they would want you to become.

Fourth, speak their name out loud as an act of defiance against a world that struggles to make room for grief that is ongoing, visible, and rooted in love. Your child's name deserves to be heard, their life deserves to be remembered, and your love for them deserves to be honored and expressed openly without apology. Every time you say their name in conversation, you declare that they lived, that they mattered, that they are still loved by someone who will never stop being their parent.

Fifth, find your people, the community of others who understand the language of loss because they have walked the same impossible path. These are not the ones who try to fix you with well-meaning advice but the parents who know the ache that lives in your arms, who can sit with you in the darkness without trying to turn on lights you are not ready for. This community becomes your lifeline, proof that you are not alone in carrying a weight no one should have to carry at all.

Sixth, when you are ready and not before, channel your love into purpose by discovering how your child's life and death can make a difference for other families walking similar paths. This might mean formal advocacy work or simple acts of kindness that reflect what their love taught you about what really matters. The transformation from surviving grief to channeling it into meaningful action gives your pain a place to go beyond your own heart, honoring your child while serving others who desperately need what you have learned.

Finally, remember that you never have to let go in order to move forward. The goal is not to get over your child but to learn to carry them with you in ways that honor both their memory and your own need to continue living. Your love for them is permanent and unbreakable, creating a bond that death cannot sever and time cannot diminish. This love becomes your compass, guiding you toward choices and actions that prove their life had meaning extending far beyond their death.

The way forward is not linear or predictable, and it does not have a destination where you can declare yourself healed or recovered. Living with grief becomes a daily discipline of allowing opposing truths to coexist, carrying the weight of their absence while still moving forward, honoring deep sorrow while recognizing your strength, and grieving what can never be recovered while staying present to what still lives within you.

Your survival becomes a testament to their life, proof that they were loved so completely that losing them could not destroy the parent who loved them. Every day you choose to keep living, every moment you find meaning in your continued existence, every action you take that honors their memory while serving your own wellbeing, you are demonstrating that love is stronger than death and that some bonds cannot be broken by anything as final as physical separation.

The actionable love that paves your way forward transforms grief from something that happens to you into something you do actively and intentionally. You choose to remember rather than forget, to speak rather than remain silent, to connect rather than isolate, to serve rather than only survive. These choices do not eliminate your pain, but they give your pain purpose, direction, and the power to create healing for others who need what you have learned through surviving the unsurvivable.

Your child's love created your grief, and that same love will carry you forward into whatever comes next. The way forward is illuminated by their memory, guided by their spirit, and sustained by a connection that transcends physical presence and proves that some loves are so deep they become eternal, so strong they can survive anything, so pure they can transform even the deepest sorrow into a source of light for others walking through their own darkness.

At its core, this entire book is an invitation to name and honor what your heart is already doing After the Goodbye: holding love for a child who will always be yours, gently releasing the guilt and blame that were never meant to live in your body, and learning, in your own time, what it means to love forward in a life forever changed by their absence. You are not asked to choose one of these or to complete them in order; you are simply asked to notice them, to trust that they will rise and recede like waves, and to let them guide you one breath, one choice, one connection at a time.

As you step away from these pages and into whatever comes next, may the title itself become a soft reminder, a hand on your shoulder whispering: even after the goodbye, your love is still here, you are still here, and together you are still writing a story that did not end.

Honor your grief and child by living fully while carrying them always, by speaking their name without apology, by letting their love guide you toward choices that matter, by refusing to let death have the final word in a relationship built on bonds this deep and permanent. Your survival is their legacy, your love is their continuation, and your willingness to keep living in their honor is the most beautiful tribute you can offer to a life that was immeasurably significant.

Growing Around Grief

Society tells you that grief is something you get over. Healing is often described as something you work toward and eventually reach, but grief does not move in straight lines or reward effort with arrival. The expectation is that time will shrink your pain, that months and years will gradually reduce the weight of your loss until it becomes manageable, tucked away in a corner of your heart where it can exist without disrupting your daily life. This is not how grief works. Grief is a life sentence.

Grief is not something you conquer, overcome, or move past. It is not a temporary visitor that overstays its welcome but eventually packs up and leaves. Grief is permanent, a fixed point within you that will always remain the same size. Your love for your child created this grief, and that love does not shrink with time, so neither does the grief that proves how deep that love runs.

But there is another way grief can live within you, one that allows survival and, over time, the possibility of meaning: you do not move past your grief, you learn how to grow around it.

Picture your grief as a small circle, dense, dark, and unchanging. Now picture your life as a larger circle that surrounds it. In the beginning, these circles are the same size. Your grief takes up all the space available, leaving little room for anything else. Every breath, every thought, every moment of your existence is consumed by the reality of your loss.

As time passes, your grief remains exactly the same size, but your life, the outer circle, begins to expand. Slowly, carefully, you build new experiences around the edges of your grief. You learn to hold joy alongside sorrow, hope alongside despair, laughter alongside tears. Your grief never gets smaller, but your capacity to hold other things grows larger. This is growing with and around grief, and it is the only path forward that honors both your love for your child and your need to love forward with purpose.

Grief Doesn't Shrink Over Time

The first truth you must understand is that your grief will never shrink, and this is not a failure of healing or a sign that something is wrong with you. Your grief is the exact size and shape of your love for your child, and that love is permanent and unchanging. Expecting grief to diminish over time is like expecting your love to fade, and you know instinctively that your love for your child will never be less than it is right now, in this moment.

When Michael died, well-meaning people told me that time would heal my wounds, that eventually the pain would lessen, and I would be able to remember him without the crushing weight of sorrow. They meant to offer comfort, but their words felt like a betrayal because I did not want my grief to shrink. My grief was proof of my love, evidence that Michael had mattered, a testament to the bond between us that death could not break.

The idea that grief should diminish over time comes from a fundamental misunderstanding of what grief is. Society treats grief like an injury that should heal, a problem that should be solved, a temporary disruption that should resolve itself with enough time and effort. But grief is not a wound that closes; it is love that has nowhere to go in the traditional sense, love that must find new channels and new expressions now that its original recipient exists only in memory and spirit.

Your grief is as permanent as your love because it is your love, transformed by loss but never diminished by it. The ache in your arms when you long to hold your child, the tears that come without warning when you hear their name, the way your heart contracts when you see other families living the life you were supposed to have, these are not symptoms of incomplete healing. They are expressions of complete love, love so deep and real that it cannot be contained by the boundaries of life and death.

Understanding that grief does not shrink gives you permission to stop trying to get over your loss and start learning to live with it. It frees you from the exhausting work of trying to minimize your pain or pretend that time is making everything better when your experience tells you otherwise. It allows you to honor your grief as sacred rather than treating it as pathological, to see it as a lifelong companion rather than a temporary burden.

This permanence of grief can feel overwhelming when you first understand it, especially in those early days when the pain is so intense you cannot imagine carrying it for the rest of your life. But grief that does not shrink is also grief that does not fade, which means your connection to your child remains as strong and real as it was on the day they died. Your love for them will never be relegated to the past tense; it will always be present, active, guiding your choices and shaping who you become.

The central struggle you face is learning how to live in a world where your child no longer exists while you still do. When your child died, you lost more than their physical presence; you lost the version of yourself who existed before the loss. The world became unfamiliar, your identity shattered, and even your body remembered the absence in ways that felt impossible to bear. Every breath, every sunrise, every quiet moment became a confrontation with the impossible question: How do I keep living when my child does not?

This is not just emotional pain; it is existential disorientation that touches every layer of who you are. Your sense of identity as a parent who can no longer parent in traditional ways. Your sense of safety in a world where the worst thing imaginable happened. Your sense of belonging when no one else seems to understand the weight you carry. Your relationship to time when the world keeps moving but you remain frozen in the moment everything changed. Your relationship to love when you must learn to love someone you cannot touch, hold, or protect in the ways that once felt natural and necessary.

Society is deeply uncomfortable with grief, especially the grief of child loss, because it forces people to confront their own vulnerability and the reality that terrible things can happen to good people without reason or warning. Friends may fall silent, not knowing what to say or afraid of saying the wrong thing. People may disappear entirely, unable to bear witness to pain they cannot fix. Your grief becomes too heavy, too much, too long for others who want you to return to the person you were before, not understanding that person no longer exists.

The result is a profound loneliness that can feel even more isolating than the original loss. You find yourself exiled from the world you once belonged to, carrying knowledge that others cannot understand and pain that others cannot witness without discomfort. Your grief makes others uncomfortable because it reminds them that loss is always possible, that love does not guarantee safety, that some sorrows cannot be fixed with time or positive thinking or well-meaning advice.

But your grief is not too much, and your love is not too big. The problem is not that your grief is excessive; the problem is that the world has forgotten how to hold space for the deepest expressions of human love and loss. Your grief is the appropriate response to losing someone who meant everything to you. It is proof that your child's life had immense value, that your bond was real and powerful, that love like yours does not simply disappear when its object is no longer physically present.

The death of your child fractured your identity in ways that extend far beyond the immediate grief for your child. You are no longer the person you were before, and you never will be again. A mother or father who once parented through presence must now learn to parent through memory. You must figure out how to carry your child forward while rediscovering who you are in this new, unwanted life that includes their absence but not their physical presence.

Cultural narratives about grief are impatient and unrealistic, insisting that healing follows predictable stages and timelines. You may be told to be grateful for other children, to get back to work, to find closure and move forward with your life. But closure does not exist when it comes to the loss of a child. What you need is not closure but continuing bonds, a way to stay connected to your child with love, without apology, for the rest of your life.

Perhaps the most haunting fear is that your child will be forgotten by others, by the world, even by yourself as time passes and life demands your attention in other directions. You long for acknowledgment that your child was here, that they mattered, that they still matter now. You need to know that their life had meaning and impact that extends beyond their death, that their existence created ripples that continue to spread even though they are no longer here to see them.

At the heart of your struggle is a paradox that every bereaved parent lives with you are forever changed by love and loss, required to learn how to mother or father in absence, to love in a world that cannot see your child. You are not looking for answers because there are no answers that can make sense of such loss. You are looking for language to express what feels inexpressible, for reflection that honors the complexity of your experience, for belonging with others who understand the weight you carry, for proof that what you feel is survivable and that love, even after death, still has a place to go.

Understanding that grief does not shrink is the foundation for everything else, you must learn about surviving child loss. It gives you permission to stop trying to get better in ways that diminish your connection to your child and start learning to grow stronger in ways that honor that connection. It allows you to see your grief as evidence of love rather than evidence of pathology, as a sacred trust rather than a burden to be overcome.

Your grief is not the enemy; it is the evidence of your love. It is not something to be conquered but something to be carried, not something to be cured but something to be honored as the deepest expression of the most important relationship in your life. When you stop trying to make your grief smaller and start learning to make your life bigger, you begin the real work of growing around grief rather than trying to grow past it.

The Non-Linearity of Grief

Grief is not a series of neat stages you progress through like checkpoints on a predetermined path toward healing. It is not a process with a clear endpoint where recovery is waiting for you once enough effort has been applied, not a tunnel you walk through with light guaranteed at the end.

Grief is a roller coaster that can plunge you back into acute pain without warning, even years after your child died, even when you thought you were doing better, even when others expect you to be past the worst of it. This roller coaster has no schedule, no predictable pattern, no consideration for your plans or your progress or your desperate need for the pain to follow some kind of logical progression that you can understand and manage.

Anniversaries, birthdays, and holidays are landmines of pain that you must face year after year, but the waves of grief can also hit during the most ordinary moments, triggered by things so small and unexpected that you cannot prepare for them or protect yourself from their impact.

A song playing in the grocery store or a scent that reminds you of them. Seeing a child or adult of a similar age to what your child would be now, living the life your child will never have. These triggers can send you spiraling back into grief so raw it feels as fresh as the first day, so overwhelming you wonder if you have learned nothing at all about how to survive this loss.

Understanding the non-linear nature of grief is crucial because it frees you from the expectation that you should be better by now, that you should have moved past certain stages of pain, that you should be making steady progress toward some version of normal that feels manageable and predictable. There is no timeline for grief, no schedule that your heart must follow, no deadline by which you must achieve acceptance or peace or whatever others think healing should look like.

The roller coaster of grief has sharp drops that come without warning, moments when the reality of your loss hits you with the same force it had in those first horrible days. You might be having what feels like a good day, managing your responsibilities and maybe even experiencing moments of something that resembles normalcy, when suddenly the ground gives way beneath you and you find yourself back in that place of raw, desperate pain where breathing feels impossible and survival seems unlikely.

These drops are not evidence that you are going backward or that your healing is incomplete. They are proof that your love for your child is as strong as ever, that your bond with them remains unbroken by time or distance or the world's expectations that you should be moving on. The intensity of these waves demonstrates the depth of your connection, not the failure of your recovery.

There are also unexpected moments of peace, times when the roller coaster levels out and you can catch your breath, remember who you are beyond your grief, and glimpse the possibility that life might hold meaning and even joy again. These moments can feel like betrayal at first, as if experiencing anything other than constant sorrow means you are forgetting your child or minimizing the significance of your loss.

But these respites are not betrayal; they are your life expanding around your grief, creating space for other experiences and emotions to coexist with your love and sorrow. They are proof that you are growing stronger, not because your grief is diminishing but because your capacity to hold multiple realities at once is increasing. You can miss your child desperately while also feeling grateful for the time you had together. You can ache with longing while also appreciating the beauty of a sunset.

You can cry for what was lost while also smiling at a memory that brings warmth instead of only pain.

The non-linearity of grief means that progress is not measured by the absence of difficult days but by your growing ability to survive them when they come. Success is not reaching a place where grief no longer affects you; success is learning to ride the roller coaster without being destroyed by its sudden turns and drops. It is developing the skills and support systems that help you navigate the waves when they crash over you, knowing that they will eventually recede even if you cannot see how that is possible when you are in the middle of them.

Some days you will feel like you are drowning, pulled under by grief so completely it fills every cell in your body. Other days you will feel like you are floating, held up by memories and love and the gradual recognition that your child's death, while it changed everything, did not end your capacity for life and meaning and connection. Most days will fall somewhere between these extremes, mixing sorrow and strength in proportions that shift without warning and cannot be predicted or controlled.

This unpredictability can feel grueling and overwhelming, especially when you are trying to function in a world that expects consistency and reliability. You might have to cancel plans because a grief wave hits at the wrong moment. You might find yourself crying in inappropriate places or struggling to concentrate on tasks that used to be automatic. You might have to explain to employers, friends, and family members that grief does not follow their timelines or accommodate their expectations about when you should be feeling better.

Learning to allow for the ebb and flow of grief, the sudden drops, and unexpected moments of peace, is part of learning to live with loss rather than trying to overcome it. It means accepting that some days will be harder than others for reasons you cannot predict or control. It means building flexibility into your life so that you can respond to your needs as they arise rather than forcing yourself to maintain a schedule or pace that ignores the reality of your emotional experience.

The roller coaster of grief also means that healing is not a destination you reach but a process you engage with for the rest of your life. There will always be moments when the loss hits you with unexpected force, when the absence of your child feels as shocking and impossible as it did in the beginning. But there will also be times when their memory brings comfort instead of only pain, when their love feels like a source of strength rather than a reminder of what you cannot have.

The goal is not to get off the roller coaster but to learn to ride it with grace, to develop the inner resources that help you navigate its ups and downs without being completely overwhelmed by its intensity. This might mean creating support systems that you can access quickly when grief waves hit. It might mean developing coping strategies that help you breathe through the worst moments. It might mean learning to recognize the signs that a difficult period is approaching so you can prepare yourself as much as possible.

Most importantly, understanding the non-linear nature of grief gives you permission to feel whatever you are feeling at any given moment without judgment or the pressure to be somewhere else emotionally. If you are having a terrible day five years after your child died, that does not mean you are stuck, broken, or failing to heal properly. It means you are human, loving someone you cannot hold, learning to live with a loss that will always be part of your story.

The roller coaster of grief is not something you will ever master completely, but it is something you can learn to ride and eventually even find meaning within. Each time you move through a wave of intense sorrow, each time you discover that you can feel joy without betraying your child's memory, each time you realize that your love for them continues to guide and sustain you even in their absence, you are growing around your grief in ways that honor both your loss and your resilience.

Finding Joy Without Guilt

For many bereaved parents, the idea of laughing again or feeling genuine happiness can feel almost unreachable, not because joy disappears, but because guilt often arrives alongside it, questioning whether a loving parent is allowed to feel anything good after their child has died. It can feel like the deepest betrayal of your child's memory to smile at a joke, to enjoy a meal, to find pleasure in a sunset or a song or a moment of connection with another person.

This guilt is one of the cruelest aspects of grief because it robs you of the very experiences that might help you survive your loss and honor your child's life. It turns every moment of lightness into evidence that you are a terrible parent, every laugh into proof that you are forgetting what matters most, every experience of beauty or connection into a betrayal of the love that defines who you are.

But within the framework of growing around grief, joy is not a sign that you are forgetting your child or minimizing the significance of your loss. Joy is a sign that your life is expanding, that you are creating space around your grief for other experiences and emotions to coexist with your sorrow. When joy peeks through again, however tentatively and briefly, it is not because you have forgotten your child but because their love has carved out space for you to keep living.

Your child's love does not demand your perpetual sadness. The love between you was not built on suffering but on connection, on the desire for each other's happiness and wellbeing, on hopes and dreams that included joy and laughter and all the beautiful experiences that make life worth living. That love does not disappear when your child dies, and it does not transform into something that requires you to remain forever trapped in the darkest corners of your grief.

When you experience a moment of joy, however small and unexpected, you can consciously reframe it as evidence of your child's ongoing love for you. Instead of thinking, "How can I be happy when my child is dead?" you can think, "This joy exists because of the love my child gave me. It does not erase them; it honors them." This shift in perspective transforms guilt into gratitude, betrayal into tribute, evidence of forgetting into proof of remembering.

The first time you laugh after your child dies; it might feel like the most shocking thing that has ever happened to you. Your body might shudder from the sound, your mind might flood with guilt and confusion, your heart might ache with the contradiction of feeling lightness amid the heaviest loss imaginable. This is normal and expected. Your system is learning to hold multiple realities at once, to be both grieving and living, both heartbroken and capable of moments that feel like healing.

These moments of joy are often unexpected and fleeting at first, appearing without warning and disappearing just as abruptly. You might find yourself smiling at a memory of your child before the weight of their absence crashes down again. You might laugh at something funny on television before remembering that they will never watch movies or share jokes with you. You might feel a moment of peace while watching a sunrise before the reality of facing another day without them overwhelms you again.

Rather than fighting these moments or feeling guilty about them, you can learn to receive them as gifts from your child, evidence that their love continues to flow through your life in ways that bring light even in the midst of darkness. These moments are proof that your expanded life can hold both profound sorrow and genuine happiness simultaneously, that growing around grief means making room for the full spectrum of human experience rather than limiting yourself to only the darkest emotions.

Joy after loss often looks different than joy before loss. It might be quieter, more precious, tinged with awareness of how instantly everything can change. It might come mixed with tears, bittersweet rather than purely happy, complicated by the knowledge that your child cannot share in these moments with you in the ways you had planned and hoped. But this different quality does not make it less valid or less important; it makes it sacred, a testament to your resilience and your child's enduring impact on your capacity for life and love.

Finding joy without guilt requires practice and patience with yourself as you learn to navigate these complex emotions. It helps to have a prepared response for the guilt when it arises, a conscious way of redirecting your thoughts toward honoring your child rather than punishing yourself. When you catch yourself feeling guilty about a moment of happiness, you can remind yourself that your child would want you to experience joy, that their love was never conditional on your suffering, that surviving and even thriving is the greatest tribute you can offer to their memory.

This practice also involves surrounding yourself with people who understand that grief and joy can coexist, who do not expect you to choose between honoring your child and living your life. You need support from those who recognize that laughing does not mean you have forgotten, that experiencing pleasure does not mean you are over your loss, that finding meaning and beauty in life is not a betrayal of your child but a reflection of the love they gave you and the person they helped you become.

Some bereaved parents find it helpful to explicitly invite their child to be present during moments of joy, to consciously include them in experiences of beauty, connection, or celebration. This might mean speaking to them silently during a beautiful sunset, imagining their presence during a family gathering, or dedicating moments of happiness to their memory. These practices can help bridge the gap between grief and joy, making it possible to experience both simultaneously without feeling like you are betraying your love for your child.

The guilt around joy often stems from the fear that if you stop suffering constantly, the world will forget your child or think that their death was not significant. But your suffering is not what keeps your child's memory alive; your love is what keeps their memory alive. And that love can be expressed through joy just as powerfully as it can be expressed through sorrow, through living fully just as meaningfully as through grieving deeply.

As you practice allowing joy without guilt, you may discover that these moments of lightness enhance your connection to your child rather than diminishing it. When you experience something beautiful, you might find yourself wishing you could share it with them, feeling their presence more strongly rather than less. When you laugh, you might hear echoes of the laughter you shared or imagine the laughter you would have shared if they had lived longer. When you feel grateful for life's gifts, you might recognize that your capacity for gratitude was deepened by your love for them and your awareness of how precious and fragile life really is.

Joy without guilt is not about forgetting your child or pretending that their death does not matter. It is about honoring their life by continuing to live yours, about expressing your love for them through your willingness to remain open to beauty and connection and meaning even in their physical absence. It is about understanding that your child's greatest wish for you would not be perpetual suffering but continued life, not endless sorrow but enduring love that finds expression through the full range of human experience.

The moments of joy that come as you grow around your grief are proof that love is stronger than death, that your child's impact on your life extends beyond their dying to include their ongoing influence on your capacity for happiness and hope. These moments do not erase your grief or minimize your loss; they demonstrate that your life is big enough to hold both the deepest sorrow and the most unexpected joy, both the reality of death and the persistence of love.

Expanding Your Life Around Unchanging Loss

You have encountered one of the most misunderstood truths about grief: it does not shrink over time. Your grief is the exact size and shape of your love for your child, and that love is permanent. The profound shift that happens is not that grief gets smaller, it is that your life, slowly and painfully, begins to grow around it.

This chapter has challenged everything you may have been told about healing. Society wants you to "get over it," to move through neat stages toward recovery, to return to who you were before. But you have learned that recovery implies returning to a previous state that no longer exists and cannot be reclaimed. Instead, you are learning to build a new life that can hold both grief and joy, both absence and presence, both the reality of death and the permanence of love.

Picture two circles: your grief as a dense, unchanging inner circle, and your life as the larger circle that surrounds it. In the beginning, these circles are the same size. Grief fills all available space, leaving room for nothing else. Every breath, every thought, every waking moment is consumed by loss. But over time, not through any lessening of grief but through the slow accumulation of new experiences, the outer circle expands. Your capacity to hold other realities alongside your grief gradually increases.

You have learned about the non-linearity of grief, how it operates not as a straight path toward healing but as a roller coaster with sudden drops and unexpected moments of peace. Years after your child's death, something small, a song, a scent, the sight of another child, can plunge you back into pain so raw it feels brand new. These moments do not mean you are going backward or that something is wrong with you. They mean your love is as strong as ever, your bond as unbroken by time.

You have discovered that progress is not measured by the absence of difficult days but by your growing ability to survive them when they come. Success is not reaching a place where grief no longer affects you, it is learning to ride the roller coaster without being destroyed by its turns. It is building the skills and support systems that help you navigate the waves when they crash over you, trusting that they will eventually recede even when you cannot see how.

The world's discomfort with your ongoing grief has become more pronounced as time passes. People expect you to be better by now. They grow impatient with your continued sadness. Your grief becomes too heavy, too much, too long for others who want you to return to the person you were before. But you have learned that their expectations are not your responsibility. There is no timeline for grief, no schedule your heart must follow, no deadline by which you must achieve some version of normal that others can accept.

You are learning to protect yourself from comparisons, from the voices that insist you should be further along than you are. Every grief journey is unique. What worked for someone else may not work for you. How long it took another person to "feel better" has no bearing on your process. You are writing your own map through this territory, and only you can know what pace your heart can sustain.

This chapter has shown you that growing around grief means developing capacity to hold multiple truths simultaneously. You can miss your child desperately while also feeling grateful for the time you had together. You can ache with longing while also appreciating beauty in the world. You can cry for what was lost while also smiling at a memory that brings warmth instead of only pain. These are not contradictions; they are the complex reality of a heart learning to hold both/and instead of either/or.

You have begun to understand that your grief is not your enemy. It is evidence of love, proof that your child's life had immense value, a testament to a bond so powerful that death could not break it. When you stop trying to make grief smaller and start learning to make your life bigger, you begin the real work of growing around rather than moving past.

The goal is not happiness that erases sadness. It is wholeness that can contain both. It is a life large enough to hold your grief without being defined entirely by it, spacious enough to honor your child's memory while also embracing new experiences, strong enough to carry both the weight of loss and the possibility of meaning.

The beautiful truth about growing around grief is that it allows you to honor both your child's death and your own life, both your sorrow and your strength, both what ended and what continues. You learn that you can be both grieving and living, both broken and becoming, both forever changed by loss and still capable of growth and meaning and unexpected moments of grace.

Here are the specific actionable steps for integrating loss into your new life:

Draw two circles on a piece of paper, one small circle inside a larger one. Label the inner circle "Grief" and the outer circle "My Life." Keep this drawing somewhere you can see it regularly as a visual reminder that your grief remains constant while your life grows around it. When you feel overwhelmed by sorrow, look at this image and remember that you are not trying to make the inner circle smaller but to make the outer circle bigger, creating more space for experiences and emotions beyond your grief.

When an unexpected grief wave hits, name it out loud by saying: "This is the roller coaster. This feeling will pass." This simple acknowledgment helps you remember that intense waves of sorrow are normal parts of the grieving process rather than signs that something is wrong or that you are not healing properly. The wave will recede, just as it has every other time, even when you cannot imagine how that is possible in the moment.

The next time you experience a moment of joy, however small, consciously tell yourself: "This joy exists because of the love my child gave me. It does not erase them." Practice this reframing every time guilt tries to steal your moments of lightness, understanding that your child's love created your capacity for happiness and that experiencing joy is a way of honoring their ongoing impact on your life rather than betraying their memory.

Create a weekly ritual that consciously includes your child in your current life, such as lighting a candle while you tell them about your week, looking at their photo while you drink your morning coffee, or wearing something that reminds you of them during family gatherings. This practice keeps them present in your routine rather than relegating their memory to special occasions or moments of intense grief.

When someone tells you that you should be "over this by now" or that it is time to "move on," respond with: "I'm not trying to get over my child. I'm learning to carry them with me." This response educates others about the reality of grief while also reinforcing for yourself that your goal is integration rather than elimination, carrying forward rather than moving past.

Identify one way that your child's death has changed you for the better, such as increased compassion, deeper appreciation for life's fragility, or stronger connections with other bereaved parents. Write this down and return to it when you struggle to find any meaning in your loss, understanding that growth and wisdom can emerge from tragedy without the tragedy being necessary or welcome.

Finally, give yourself permission to have both terrible days and surprisingly good days without judgment about either experience. Your grief does not follow a schedule, and your healing does not follow a timeline. Some days you will feel crushed by sorrow; other days you will feel carried by love. Both experiences are valid expressions of your ongoing relationship with your child and your ongoing process of learning to live in their honor.

Growing around grief is the work of a lifetime, an ongoing process of learning to hold love and loss simultaneously while building a life that honors both your child's memory and your own continued existence. It is not about finding closure or achieving some final state of peace, but about developing the strength and wisdom to carry your grief with grace while remaining open to all the beauty and meaning that life continues to offer, even in the midst of the deepest sorrow.

Your grief is not too much, and your love is not too big. Both are exactly the right size for the relationship you shared with your child, and both will guide you forward into whatever comes next in your journey of learning to live fully while honoring someone who cannot live alongside you in the traditional sense. The love never dies, and neither does your capacity to grow around the grief that proves how deep that love runs. You are not alone in this.

ABOUT THE AUTHOR

Dr. Maureen C. Rubalcaba is a bereaved mother, writer, and certified grief coach who teaches and guides from the sacred ground of lived experience. After the sudden death of her infant son, Michael Simon Chavez, her world fell silent in a way only a parent who has lost a child can understand. In the aftermath, she entered the long, uncharted terrain of learning how to survive a life she never chose, how to carry love without a body to hold, and how to remain a mother when her child could no longer be seen.

In the silence that followed Michael's death and after the goodbye, Dr. Rubalcaba discovered that grief was not something to fix or move beyond, but something to listen to. Her own journey through devastation, guilt, fear of judgment, and enduring love became the foundation for both her writing and her work with other bereaved parents. She writes not as an observer of grief, but as someone who lives within it by honoring the truth that love does not end with death, it changes form.

Dr. Rubalcaba is the creator of the HeartHeld Method™, a compassionate framework that gently supports bereaved parents as they navigate grief without guilt, self-blame, or the pressure to "heal" on anyone else's timeline. Her work affirms that grief is not pathology, weakness, or something to overcome, but love that continues in a world that no longer makes space for it. Through writing, coaching, and sacred witnessing, she creates environments where parents are invited to speak their child's name freely, honor continuing bonds, and rediscover meaning and purpose while keeping their child's presence woven into their lives.

After the Goodbye was born from this lived truth. It is both a testimony and a companion written for parents who are still breathing even when they are unsure how, who are learning to live forward while holding their child close in memory, body, and soul. Dr. Rubalcaba believes that surviving child loss does not mean leaving love behind but learning how to carry it differently.

If you are walking this path, may you find in these pages a steady hand, a shared language for your loss, and the reassurance that your love still has somewhere to go.

YOU ARE NOT ALONE

Grief doesn't have an expiration date and neither does love. I help parents navigate grief without guilt or fear of judgment so that you can release self-blame and love forward with purpose and meaning after child loss. Learn more about *The HeartHeld Method*™ courses and programs at www.chingonaservices.com.

Connect with me at:
drarubalcaba@chingonaservices.com
Instagram: @thehearteldmethod

www.ingramcontent.com/pod-product-compliance
Lightning Source LLC
Chambersburg PA
CBHW061332140726
47997CB00003B/958